The CIO
and the Democratic Party

The CIO
and the Democratic Party

by Fay Calkins

 THE UNIVERSITY OF CHICAGO PRESS

THE UNIVERSITY OF CHICAGO PRESS, CHICAGO 60637
THE UNIVERSITY OF CHICAGO PRESS, LTD., LONDON

© 1952 by The University of Chicago. All rights reserved
Published 1952. Midway Reprint 1975
Printed in the United States of America

International Standard Book Number: 0-226-09098-1

To my father
who first stimulated my
political curiosity

Preface

BOTH the friends and the critics of organized labor have had a great deal to say about the political activities of unions in modern American society. Outside the ranks of unions, questions have been raised regarding the appropriate role of labor in the political life of the nation; and within the labor movement itself the nature and extent of political action have often been an issue leading to sharp controversy. Despite keen interest in this subject, however, there has been very little realistic and systematic analysis of the relationships between organized labor and our political parties. This volume, we feel, makes a contribution to knowledge in this vital area of political science. Miss Calkins has presented, from the viewpoint of the political scientist, a thought-provoking appraisal of various types of relationships between the CIO and the Democratic party in the 1950 local, state, and congressional elections.

In this study Miss Calkins deals with some fundamental questions: What alternative kinds of relationships are possible between labor as an interest group and a political party? What forces determine the choice of a particular kind of relationship? What compromise must labor make in seeking to work with or within a political party? What problems of tactics and timing do union leaders face when they seek to mobilize their limited political resources to vie with party leaders in nominating and electing candidates? Under what conditions is the union able to exercise controlling influence over the party, and, conversely, when is the party able to get the union to conform to its program and policy? Miss Calkins provides us with fresh data and insights on such problems.

The material for this study was based largely on extensive interviews with union and party officials—the men of action who had to make down-to-earth decisions in the 1950 campaigns. The five case studies of union-party relationships, which provide the empirical basis for the analysis, are live and authentic. For this reason, union leaders, party officials, and members of the general public who are concerned with modern political developments will undoubtedly find this volume as interesting and stimulating as will the political scientist and the student of industrial relations.

For the last four years Miss Calkins has been associated with the Industrial Relations Center as a staff member and with the Department of Political Science of the University of Chicago as a graduate student and research fellow. The influence of organized groups on American politics has been an important area of research for the Department of Political Science for many years. One of the major continuing research programs of the Industrial Relations Center is concerned with the social, economic, and political impact of unionism on modern American institutions. *The CIO and the Democratic Party* is the first project in the area of labor and politics to be completed under the joint direction of the department and the Center.

FREDERICK H. HARBISON
Professor of Industrial Relations

AVERY LEISERSON
Associate Professor of Political Science

UNIVERSITY OF CHICAGO

Table of Contents

List of Illustrations

List of Tables

I *Parties and Pressure Groups*

MENTION the word "pressure group" to an average American, and a shudder chills his spine. Perhaps, like a primitive man before his thunder-god, he feels he is the victim of forces he cannot control or even understand—"big business," "labor bosses," "special interests." To him these are forces remote from his family dinner table and the boys in the shop. Yet, in some mysterious way, these organized interests stand between him and his government; they seem "undemocratic." When the newspapers tell him that "labor has captured the Democratic party" or his local union president tells him that "the Republican party is a tool of the National Association of Manufacturers (NAM)," he gets angry.

Thunder became less terrifying when man understood what caused it and learned to channel lightning. Interest groups may likewise seem less sinister—they may even prove useful—as citizens come to know more about how they operate and how they can be used democratically in American political life.

Exploration into the life and habits of interest groups has just begun. Most frequently studied have been the lobbies which interest groups use to impress legislators. Congress has already investigated itself several times on this score. More recently, political scientists have begun to trace the interplay of pressures on administrative agencies. But other important political institutions are still a virgin field of inquiry. How do inter-

1

est groups make themselves felt in our courts and in our political parties, for example?

This study is a preliminary expedition into one of these untried fields. It asks: How do interest groups bring pressure to bear on political parties?

The Problem

This is no academic question, interesting only to political scientists. It is a practical question to the voter in the booth, the merchant in the chamber of commerce, and the worker in his union meeting. It is these ordinary citizens who can use, or be used by, pressure groups.

The question of parties and pressure groups may occur to any voter as he walks to the polls on election morning. In his heart he wonders, "Am I just the pawn of a lot of 'interests,' operating quietly behind the scenes?" "Who are these 'interests,' anyway?" "How much power do they have?" "How do they operate?" In his election-day mood a voter may be all for ridding his party of these sinister "special interests."

But the question of parties and pressure groups may occur to him in quite another form as he rides to the chamber of commerce or union hall on meeting night. He may feel worked up about corporation taxes or price controls. He wonders to himself, "How can we get the party to nominate a man who will support these issues?" "How can we get that man elected?" In his workday mood a voter may be all for promoting his own interest group.

Both these moods are legitimate for a citizen living in a democracy. He should feel free both to build and to regulate pressure groups. But his effectiveness in doing so will depend on knowing something about pressure groups and how they operate in political parties.

A Method of Study

Politics is neither run nor understood in terms of abstract principles. It is one of those lively subjects which can only be studied on the spot and appreciated in the concrete. To capture "political life," therefore, this study is presented in the form of five actual case histories of relationships established between an interest group and a political party.

The case-study method has admitted limitations. There are two major parties, hundreds of pressure groups, a hundred and seventy-five years of elections, and thousands of communities in this country. No five cases can possibly be representative. The cases selected for study here illustrate different types of relationships established between one interest group, the Political Action Committee (PAC) and one party, the Democratic party. PAC is by no means the only, or even the most influential, interest group at work on the Democratic party. It is merely one of many. Nor does PAC work only on the Democratic party. Like any interest group, it brings pressure wherever it thinks it can produce an effect. These five cases cannot even be considered typical of PAC. The five PAC's studied here were deliberately selected as being among the most active in the country, in order to illustrate the pressure group–party relationship at its height. Most local PAC's have not developed to the point described here.

The first case is the story of what happened in Ohio in 1950. Robert Taft was up for re-election to the Senate. CIO regarded him as the kingpin of antilabor forces in Congress and quite naturally wanted to retire him from this post. But that was no easy task. Under the circumstances, organized labor felt that the most realistic method of defeating Taft was to campaign vigorously for his Democratic opponent, Joseph Ferguson.

PAC thus *supplemented* the work of the Democratic party. The second case took place in Steubenville, Ohio. Here Wayne Hays, a "good" man from CIO's standpoint, was up for re-election to the House of Representatives. He was supported in Jefferson County by a Democratic machine under the leadership of an energetic young party chairman, "friendly" to labor. The congressional race was so close in Jefferson County in 1950 that PAC's independent political organization was able to shift the victory from Republican to Democratic. PAC was thus in a position not merely to supplement the Democratic party. It could demand some concessions from the party because it held a *balance of power*. Chicago, the third case, presented a far tougher problem to PAC. Not only was the Democratic machine here strong, but it was "unfriendly." Labor felt that it could neither supplement the Democratic candidate nor balance power, so it entered its own independent candidate in the Democratic primary. If its *primary challenge* had been successful, PAC would have had a Democratic candidate of its own choosing on the final ballot. It would have taken one important political decision out of the hands of the machine.

In Rockford, Illinois, PAC tried a wholly different method of influencing the Democratic party. Instead of building an independent political organization with which it could supplement, balance, or challenge the Democratic party, labor entered and took control of the county party itself. Through this *partisan relationship* it gained considerable influence over internal party decisions, even though it was not able to elect its candidate to Congress. In Michigan, PAC tried this partisan approach on a state-wide basis. In coalition with several like-minded interest groups, it took over the important offices of a weak and reactionary state party and changed it into an active liberal organization able to elect Mennen Williams as governor.

These cases may not be fully representative of interest group-party relationships. But they do have the advantage of reducing the problem to a manageable size. The author was able to go and take a firsthand look at PAC in various relationships to the party in these communities. She could thus catch some of the things that politicians never write down. The material presented here was gathered on the spot from actual participation in the political campaign or from interviews with PAC and party workers while the campaign was still "hot" in their minds. Newspaper accounts, election statistics, and interviews with neutral observers also helped in gathering and weighing information. What the case method loses in representativeness it catches in concreteness.

Concepts: A Party, an Interest Group, Their Relationship

Like United Nations delegates, people interested in politics suffer for lack of a common language. The word "party," for example, brings different images to different minds. The expression "pressure group" conjures up a wide variety of ideas and emotions. For some of the different qualities of interest groups, there simply are no standard words, and some party relationships can be expressed only in the politicians' vernacular, such as "captured by the party." If the author and reader are to understand each other, however, they must come to agreement on what a few basic political words mean. Not that these are the only possible definitions—the author quite frankly adopts definitions which seem to explain what she saw—but they do provide a common point of departure.

First, what is a political party? The voter looking at the columns of his ballot may think he knows what the Democratic party is. But ask him to define it! Who is a party member? Is it the voter who may split his ticket and whose allegiance is a secret anyway? What is the structure of a party? Is it the active machine in Chicago or the feeble committee in rural Michigan? What are the objectives of the party? Is it the "white supremacy" demanded by Rankin in Mississippi or the civil rights demanded by a Negro ward leader in Cleveland? Out of the welter of ideas and practices that make up the Democratic party in this country, it is hard to reach a precise definition.

Parties in the United States are roughly similar in one respect, however—their basic *structure*. Both major parties are built in the form of a pyramid of precinct captains, ward leaders, county committees, state committees and conventions, and national committees and conventions. In this study voters are not considered the lowest rung of this party hierarchy, since they play no direct part in internal party decisions, except perhaps at primaries. Instead, voters are regarded as customers outside the party organization who are free to reject or purchase with their votes the candidates which the party produces.

Parties are also vaguely similar in another respect—*function*—though local party organizations may perform their functions differently or even neglect them entirely. Some party functions have to do with building and holding together the party organization itself. In this study such activities are called "internal party functions" and include: (1) selecting party candidates, (2) preparing a party platform, (3) electing party officers, (4) extending party organization, (5) disciplining internal party groups, and (6) distributing party rewards. These internal functions are usually performed only by persons inside party structure, though recently the selection of candidates and some party officers has been opened to the general public at primaries. Other party activities are concerned with selling the party candidate to a majority of voters. These are referred to as "campaign functions" and include: (1) raising campaign funds, (2) registering voters, (3) soliciting support from groups outside the party, (4) publicizing candidates, and (5) watching the polls on election day. These campaign functions can be performed by interest groups whether they have entered the structure of a party or not.

But the most interesting attribute of parties for this study is their *composition.* Who are these energetic human beings who find it worth while to man party structure and perform exacting party functions? What do they want? Few people tramp the streets with leaflets and spend their spare time ringing doorbells for personal amusement. The people who perform this grueling work have objectives in mind, sometimes good, sometimes selfish. Furthermore, since single individuals working alone hold little weight in politics, these interested people usually represent groups. *Parties are organizations of interest groups willing to pool their political efforts in order to nominate and elect to office candidates who will remember their particular interests when formulating public policy.*

But what, then, is an "interest group"? Is it merely those talkative individuals who hook their fingers into senators' buttonholes? Is a garden club an interest group? How about a family?

Groups of people often find that they have interests in common, arising from their shared experiences as Negroes, Catholics, bootblacks, or corporation lawyers. Members of such groups may not try to press their common interests at all, or they may do so only as individuals. In this case they are here referred to as an "interest grouping," a potential interest group. On the other hand, these groupings may become aware of their common desires and organize themselves in pursuit of their objectives. In this case they have become an interest group.

Some interest groups, like choral societies, can realize their objectives simply within themselves, but others, like the American Medical Association, must press outward on society to attain their ends. Many weapons, legitimate and illegitimate, are available to these pressure groups. They may use economic weapons like strikes and lockouts or psychological weapons, such as propaganda and social pressure; they may limit themselves to political weapons like lobbies, caucuses, and elections; or they may even resort to physical violence, such as arson and murder. The interest groups of concern to this study are those which have chosen one particular political-pressure weapon. *They are organizations set up to pursue the common aspirations of their members by nominating and electing sympathetic candidates to public office.*

Political interest groups must be dissected a bit and their parts named before they become fruitful specimens for study. Anyone reading the following cases will discover that the interest groups described have different goals and that their particular objectives have a profound effect on how they operate. Some of these political interest groups, like the All American Club in Rockford, wanted to elect candidates who would give them jobs. Such groups are here called "patronage-oriented." Other groups like NAM and PAC were not primarily interested in jobs—their members were profitably employed already —but they wanted to elect candidates who would promote legislation helpful to them, such as tax reductions or repeal of the Taft-Hartley Act. They were "issue-oriented." A few groups were not particularly concerned with either jobs or issues; they simply wanted candidates who were efficient and honest regardless of their political philosophy. These groups are "reform-oriented." Still other interest groups were working, not for new legislation, but for nonenforcement of existing legislation. Steubenville's gambling syndicates, for example, wanted a tolerant police force. Such groups are "protection-oriented."

Another way to dissect interest groups is according to their political resources—attributes useful in creating an electoral majority. Gambling syndicates have few voters and political workers but plenty of money. Money is such a useful commodity in the election process that the party will heed their demands. PAC has comparatively weak financial resources and few trained political workers but a large organized membership from whom it may produce a bloc of votes. Naturally, the party is interested in a group which can produce this essential ingredient in forming majorities. And, finally, a group like a Communist cell may produce few voters and small bank accounts but extraordinarily dedicated and disciplined political workers. Money, votes, and workers are the basic resources of political interest groups.

Such is the nature of parties and interest groups as conceived in this study. But why do they attract each other? Why do they form a relationship?

The consent of a majority of voters in a community is usually required to elect a candidate to office. But building a majority among individualists as rugged as most Americans is no slight accomplishment. Few interest groups have enough voters, workers, and dollars to perform this feat alone. Interest groups must pool their resources to acquire this kind of political power. But, in working together to form a majority, each interest group is forced to modify its own objectives to include those of its associates. They have to compromise and accommodate to each other. Interest groups thus provide objectives; parties provide a means of reaching these objectives. Both are essential to the election process.

But the fascination of the party process lies in the variety of changing patterns into which interest groups may combine. Looking into a party is like looking into a kaleidoscope. Are there any principles governing these patterns of pressure group–party relationship?

In general, an interest group tries to make that party combination which will give it the best chance of a majority with the least modification of its objectives. In Chicago, PAC could easily combine with the Independent Voters of Illinois (IVI), a group with liberal and reform objectives, behind a single candidate because the objectives of both groups were similar. In Rockford, PAC could combine with the All American Club because the objectives of both groups, while not similar, were compatible. A single candidate could satisfy All Americans with patronage and PAC with a liberal vote in the legislature. But PAC would find difficulty in pooling its resources with the NAM, since a single candidate would be hard put to it to vote both for and against the Taft-Hartley Act at the same time. Compatibility or incompatibility of interests is thus one factor in the arrangements which interest groups make with each other inside parties.

Another principle at work in such relationships has to do with political resources. PAC may make a happy combination with a patronage group in 1950 as the result of mutual concessions. In 1952, however, PAC may feel strong enough to "kick the other boys out." PAC is subject to the same peremptory treatment itself. As Mr. Dooley once remarked, "Politics ain't bean bag."

What are some of the ways in which interest groups relate themselves to parties? Several patterns are discernible in the following cases. Interest groups may divide their resources between two parties. In this case they are "bipartisan." Or they may expend all their efforts on one party combination. Such groups are "partisan." Some interest groups enter the structure of the party to become precinct captains or state chairmen. They thus establish an "internal party relationship." Others build their own separate political organization, which they swing now to one party, now to another. This is an "external party relationship." If an interest group builds its own political structure and runs its own candidate at a general election, it becomes a "third party." There are many modifications of these basic patterns of party relationship.

Value Judgments

Are pressure groups a bad influence in our political parties? This is like asking whether the wind is good or bad. It is good if it runs the windmill and bad if it blows the house down.

Government at its best is a procedure for recognizing and adjusting conflicting human interests in a nonviolent manner. The adjustments of interest groups inside political parties are an important part of this consensus process. Thus the author would evaluate a pressure group not by whether it attempts to influence the election process but by whether it actually represents a widespread human interest and whether it limits itself to the legitimate means of influence available in a democracy. By no means do all interest groups live up to these criteria. Small groups of men often get power out of all proportion to the human desires they represent, by tricks that only a Hitler could appreciate. But it is their content and their conduct, rather than their existence, that merit control.

II *Ohio: PAC Supplements a Campaign*

ONE of 1950's "hottest" campaigns took place in Ohio. The source of the friction was Senator Robert A. Taft, running for re-election. His political future was of no small concern, especially to issue-oriented interest groups. To CIO he was author of the "infamous" Taft-Hartley Act. To the Ohio Association for the Advancement of Colored People he was father of a voluntary fair employment practices bill which defeated an enforcible version. The Ohio Association of Manufacturers, on the other hand, found him the valiant defender of corporation tax reductions and the opponent of "burdensome" government controls. The Hotel Owners Association remembered him as the man who won them exemption from the federal minimum-wage law. It was not surprising, therefore, that these interest groups should feel anxious to participate in Taft's re-election or defeat.

The Ohio case is of interest in this study because PAC poured considerable money and effort into defeating Mr. Taft and because PAC chose, as its method of political action, simply to supplement the campaign of Taft's Democratic opponent, Joseph Ferguson. Supplementing a party campaign is one of the most common forms of PAC political action. Just how did PAC attach itself to state party structure and candidates? What influence did it have on internal party decisions and the campaign? What were the advantages and limitations of this pressure relationship from PAC's point of view? Why did it adopt this particular method?

PAC and the Ohio Democratic Party

Three structures were involved in state Democratic party functions in Ohio in 1950: the Ohio State Democratic Convention, the Democratic State Executive Committee, and the Ferguson for Senator campaign committee.

The Ohio State Democratic Convention is a biennial affair. About six hundred people attended it in 1950, including county chairmen and their assistants, members of the state executive committee, and candidates. Actually, this convention took little responsibility for state party functions. Its chief contribution was a platform and general approval of the work of the state executive committee. A few of the delegates to this convention in 1950 were CIO members—unionists who happened to be active in local politics or who had been appointed to the executive committee—but labor by no means formed a significant voting bloc inside the convention. PAC did not make a deliberate attempt to enter this party structure.

The Ohio State Democratic Committee is composed of forty-four members, two from each of the state's congressional districts, elected at primaries. This committee meets within fifteen days after the primaries to select its officers and operating committees. At this meeting it has adopted the practice of selecting fifteen additional representatives from interest groups and local party groups. These appointed members, together with the forty-four elected members, form the state executive committee, which is the major executive organ of the state party.

In 1948 and 1950 the executive committee included one CIO and one AF of L representative among its fifteen appointed members. Since the labor delegates were invited and since they formed an insignificant part of the total committee, this can hardly be considered an attempt by labor to "capture" the committee. Nevertheless, some politicians worried about it. A Democratic state senator from Cleveland fumed:

"In addition to promoting the welfare of their union through the medium of the Executive Committee, these paid employees of the union will have a strong influence upon many legislators next January because of their apparent tieup with the administration. . . . The cause of labor, though important and closely aligned to the Democratic Party, is not and never will be completely the program of the Democratic Party. . . .

"We are the party of the people and the people come from every walk of life; not merely the CIO and AFL, though Clayman and Hannah would have you believe the latter to be true" (*Cleveland Press*, May 19, 1950).

The Ohio State Democratic Committee in 1950 showed no particular enthusiasm about nominating candidates, expanding party organization, co-ordinating internal party groups, and campaigning. Some political sages explained its inactivity as the result of a bad case of internal factionalism. The committee was composed of a number of well-organized and practically autonomous county parties. Some of these county leaders displayed little love for Governor Lausche, a politician of independent strength, who dazzled voters with claims of "independence from corrupt local party machines." Despite their feelings, however, these county delegates knew where patronage came from. They duly elected a "Lausche man" chairman of the committee. This chairman took no chances with mutiny. He activated the state committee only in behalf of Lausche. The state committee office referred to itself as Lausche's campaign committee. The state party showed so little interest in other candidates that some politicos even surmised that Lausche had entered some "deal" with the Republicans: he would not press a Democrat against Senator Taft in 1950, provided that the Republicans would not press Senator Bricker against Lausche in 1952. In any case, the attitude of the state party office toward Ferguson was so cool as to be hostile.

The passivity of the state committee almost inevitably called forth an old-time politician like Ferguson who could fend for himself. As state auditor, Ferguson had been able to control about six hundred jobs for sixteen years. This gave him the nucleus of a personal organization and independent contacts with the county parties. Only such a candidate could supply the political resources and local party co-ordination necessary to run a successful primary and general election campaign.

Ferguson had to depend largely on his Ferguson for Senator Committee to promote his election in 1950. This committee was composed of his personal friends plus representatives from Cuyahoga, Franklin, and Montgomery County parties. Labor sent no representative. The committee met only six times. In view of its limited resources, it decided not to make a single co-ordinated appeal to the general public. Instead, it "farmed out" campaign responsibilities to interest groups and special campaign committees, which agreed to arouse their own membership or interest grouping. The United Labor League, a campaign committee composed of the AF of L, CIO, Mine Workers, and railway brotherhoods, undertook to contact organized workers and minority groups. The Independent Citizens Committee, composed of Americans for Democratic Action (ADA) and other liberal interest groups, set to work on independent liberals. The Church Civic League, a liberal Protestant group in Cleveland, sought to bring out Democratic church members. Farmers for Ferguson and Veterans for Ferguson were temporary committees designed to arouse rural and soldier groupings. The United Labor League was by far the most active of these interest groups.

With a few minor exceptions, therefore, PAC remained outside Ohio state Democratic party structure. Accusations that CIO had "captured" the Democratic party were unfounded. But it did conduct a rousing campaign for Ferguson among its own members. Since the party was inactive and the resources of Ferguson's other groups limited, labor did account for a good share of campaign energy. It operated as an independent interest group which happened to prefer Ferguson to Taft and therefore agreed to supplement a Democratic campaign.

PAC and Internal Party Decisions

From its outside position, how much pressure could PAC bring to bear on the internal decisions of the Democratic party?

Selecting a candidate.—When party candidates were nominated at conventions, the only interest groups to have a voice were those which could send party delegates. Since the development of the direct primary, however, interested groups either inside or outside the party can run their "favorite sons" for nomination.

The Ohio PAC had a favorite son in 1950, Murray Lincoln, a liberal prominent in the Farm Bureau. From PAC's standpoint, he was much better senatorial material than Ferguson. But Lincoln had neither a personal machine nor the support of local county parties. He did not even have the full support of the AF of L or the Farm Bureau. He would have had to depend largely on PAC to pull him through primary and general elections. Before the primary, PAC tried to get Ferguson to withdraw in favor of Lincoln. When Ferguson refused, Lincoln, with the concurrence of PAC, decided not to make the race. Lincoln and PAC reckoned that they could not muster sufficient primary votes to win such a contest. PAC, thereupon, gave up the nomination idea entirely. It told its members, "Fortunately, this year unusually well qualified men are seeking the United States senatorial nomination on the Democratic ticket. All of these candidates are committed to a policy of placing the welfare of the people ahead of the profits of special interests. . . . The Ohio CIO-PAC is making no endorsement in this race" (*Monthly Review*, March, 1950, p. 7). PAC thus had little influence on the selection of the Democratic candidate for senator.

Preparing a party platform.—The Ohio state Democratic platform receives final approval from internal party groups represented at state party conventions. Since few CIO members were delegates to this convention in 1950, PAC could not exert an influence through its vote.

External interest groups, however, are allowed to testify before the platform committee of the convention, and PAC presented its legislative demands in a document entitled "Common Cause IV." The platform committee must have given PAC's request some consideration, for the final party platform contained planks similar to those of PAC on workmen's compensation, unemployment insurance, disability benefits, industrial safety, fair employment practices, farm co-operatives, and old age assistance.

As in most states, however, the party platform was more significant in propaganda than in actual legislation. State legislators were neither selected nor disciplined according to its proposals. PAC had an influence on its contents but not on its significance.

Other internal party decisions.—Interest groups with representatives on a state party committee may have a voice in building party organization, disciplining internal factions, and distributing patronage. But, since labor was a minority of two on a state committee of fifty-nine, its voice inside the Ohio party could never rise above a whisper.

PAC and the Ferguson Campaign

What PAC lacked in internal party influence, however, it made up in campaign activity. Since the state party cared little for Ferguson and Ferguson's own committee was small, PAC knew it had to exert itself if it wanted to defeat Taft. What did PAC contribute to Ferguson? How much influence did it have on the conduct of his campaign?

Fund-raising.—Taft's campaign did not suffer from malnutrition. Democratic and PAC sources claim that the Republicans spent over $4,000,000 to elect their candidate. To face this kind of competition, Ferguson's small committee needed financial help.

Help was not forthcoming from the Democratic State Executive Committee. This body reported spending a total of $36,609.02 in 1950, none specifically for Ferguson, whose campaign expenses were therefore borne largely by the Ferguson for Senator and the special-interest-group committees. Together these committees spent a total of $230,052.78, of which the CIO contributed 34 per cent. Ferguson's campaign would have been a sorry affair without labor's funds. Groups in the United Labor League, including the CIO, AF of L, Mine Workers, railway brotherhoods, and independent unions, contributed 88 per cent of the money spent in his behalf. Democratic party sources accounted for only 4 per cent of the funds spent for him at the state level. Interested individuals gave 7 per cent (see Table 1).

Instead of following the time-honored practice of quiet in-

TABLE 1

SOURCE OF FERGUSON'S CAMPAIGN FUNDS, 1950*

Campaign Committee	Total Resources	Democratic Sources	CIO Sources	Other Labor Sources†	Individual Sources
Ferguson (personal)	$ 2,270.00				$ 2,270.00
Ferguson for Senator Committee	38,489.30	$10,000.00	$ 8,882.30	$ 7,000.00	12,607.00
Farmers for Ferguson	21,118.80		7,059.46	14,059.34	
Independent Citizens Committee	30,596.00		7,500.00	23,025.00	71.00
Church Civic League	1,500.00			1,500.00	
Labor League‡	136,078.68		55,587.74	80,490.94	
Total	$230,052.78	$10,000.00	$79,029.50	$126,075.28	$14,948.00
Per cent of total	100	4	34	54	7

* Figures compiled from: Ohio, Secretary of State, "Statements of Receipts and Expenditures." The table does not include money spent by local parties or local unions.

† Other labor sources include: AF of L unions, United Mine Workers, railway brotherhoods, and the International Association of Machinists.

‡ These figures include sums spent by Labor League groups to activate their own membership.

fluence through contributions to established party and committee groups, labor spent most of its funds itself and concentrated its propaganda efforts on its own membership. In this way it hoped to build, not the Democratic party, but an independent and maneuverable bloc of labor votes. But this method left labor's political activity exposed to the naked, and often hostile, eye of the average Ohio voter.

Publicity.—Both Republican and Democratic campaigns relied heavily on leaflets, speakers, and radio programs produced at the state level. At one time eighteen different Taft leaflets were available at Republican headquarters in Columbus. Ferguson's groups were similarly active.

The Democratic State Executive Committee mentioned Ferguson, along with other state-wide candidates, in 400,000 copies of a leaflet entitled *The Democratic Party of Ohio Proudly Presents* and in an equal number of sample ballots. The Ferguson for Senator Committee was responsible for 400,000 leaflets on *Meet Your Next Senator*, $4,000 of newspaper publicity, $9,000 of radio time, and a speakers' bureau. The Independent Citizens Committee produced 7 or 8 different leaflets and a speakers' bureau of its own. Farmers for Ferguson sent 3 issues of a tabloid newspaper to all rural boxholders. The chief contribution of Veterans for Ferguson was 25,000 copies of a leaflet entitled, *Vets, Look at the Record*.

The United Labor League outdid itself on political literature. Best known was a colorful comic book entitled *The Robert Alphonso Taft Story*, which circulated in 1,000,000 copies. The league was also responsible for a 218-page *Speakers' Handbook*, containing the details of Taft's voting record. It also issued a folder, *Because America Is Worth It*. Separate labor federations and international unions prepared their own. The state PAC, for example, distributed a special leaflet encouraging Negroes to register and vote, and the Bartenders' Union put out a reprint, *Robert A. Taft—the Record of His Twelve Year Fight against the American People*. Ferguson's virtues were extolled in innumerable local shop bulletins.

Much of labor's literature, it will be noted, was anti-Taft rather than pro-Ferguson. Since it was designed specifically for labor consumption, it could sport such provocative terms as "Phinias Moneybags" and "profit hungry." These class-conscious phrases shocked traditional politicians. The Democratic county chairman in Steubenville hesitated to use labor literature because of its limited appeal, and Taft followers literally "saw red."

Labor League publicity undoubtedly did give the campaign a "labor flavor," not because of subversive labor pressure, but simply because labor produced the most ample and vivid publicity.

Contacting interest groups.—Ferguson's campaign strategy rested largely on an attempt to reach voters through the separate interest groups to which they belonged rather than on a general appeal to the voting public. He used special campaign committees. What interest groups composed these committees? How well did they arouse the voters to whom they were directed?

The Ferguson for Senator Committee was composed largely of persons interested in Ferguson for personal or patronage reasons. The three representatives of county Democratic parties who acted on it undoubtedly had in mind the patronage at the disposal of an elected senator. Other individuals, like the campaign and publicity managers, had worked for Ferguson as auditor and presumably would have worked for him as senator. In the absence of an active state committee, the special concern of the Ferguson for Senator Committee was to arouse and co-ordinate county Democratic parties in Ferguson's behalf. This was a difficult job: county parties relied heavily on county officials for their patronage, so a candidate for senator was not their first concern. Also they relied on the governor for state patronage and so hesitated to express enthusiasm for Ferguson in view of Lausche's coolness. As a result, many patronage groups represented in local parties were not active for Ferguson.

The Independent Citizens Committee was composed of the Americans for Democratic Action and a few other liberal, issue-oriented groups among professionals and small businessmen. Henry Miller Bush, a sociology professor from Cleveland, had been their choice in the primary, and he offered to reactivate these groups in Ferguson's behalf in the general election. He established campaign offices in Cleveland and Cincinnati. Although this campaign committee worked actively among independent and liberal groups, it faced several difficulties. Such groups were not large and were confined to a few cities. Liberal interest groups were often disunited over methods of political activity, and they were not really enthusiastic about Ferguson. To them he was a "conventional politician" rather a "liberal statesman."

The Church Civic League was a permanent issue-oriented organization among Protestant liberals in Cleveland. It backed Ferguson primarily because of its concern with fair employment practices and an improved mental health program. Its leader, a clergyman, took to the stump throughout the state. The efforts of this particular group were limited by the distaste of many Protestants for political activity and by the pro-Republican activities of other Protestant groups. One Lutheran minister, for example, sent a letter to prominent Protestant clergymen, pointing out that four state-wide Democratic candidates, including Ferguson, were Catholic. The Ohio Council of Churches, while making no indorsements, notified its members of the religious affiliation of candidates. Such activities had Republican overtones.

Farmers for Ferguson and Veterans for Ferguson were not very active in contacting their respective interest groups. The farmers' committee was not, like labor's league, a spontaneous movement of interest groups for Ferguson. It was inspired and financed not by the Grange, the Farm Bureau, or rural co-operatives, but by labor. The committee made its contacts directly with rural boxholders rather than with leaders of existing farm interest groups. Veterans for Ferguson was a fleeting attempt by labor to expose Taft's record on legislation of interest to veterans, but it did not arouse much response from the American Legion, the Veterans of Foreign Wars, or even the American Veterans Committee.

The United Labor League, on the other hand, represented the spontaneous interest of various labor groups: the AF of L, CIO, Mine Workers, railway brotherhoods, and International Association of Machinists. It was self-motivated. The labor federations united only for one limited objective—the defeat of Senator Taft. Their interest in this particular project, however, was great enough not only to activate them down to the precinct level but to cause them to contact other groups as well. PAC made an effort to arouse minority, farm, and church groups.

PAC was particularly interested in activating Negroes, because it believed their economic and racial interests to be compatible with its own. A PAC study before the election indicated that there were 200,000–300,000 potential Negro voters in Ohio, concentrated in the ten largest cities. In 1948 only two-thirds of them were registered, and less than half voted.

The state PAC, therefore, appointed one full-time staff member to act as liaison with Negro groups. It issued a special leaflet encouraging Negroes to vote, and several of its field workers devoted themselves to this project. PAC's assumptions about the inactivity but the potential Democratic nature of the Negro vote seemed warranted by 1950 returns, at least in Columbus. The Democratic vote was 61 per cent in Negro wards, as compared with 53.5 per cent in white lower-income wards and 26 per cent in white upper-income wards.

For several years PAC has designated a staff member to improve its contacts with liberal farm and church groups. During 1950 he held discussion meetings of farm and industrial workers in twelve counties. PAC helped sponsor two radio series directed to farmers. These efforts, however, did not establish any real political alignments between labor and farm interest groups.

Because of the weakness of his own committee, Ferguson had to rely heavily on the support of these external interest groups. But a campaign built on special interest groups had several drawbacks. Important segments of the population were poorly contacted, and the efforts of active groups like PAC could easily be drawn to public attention by Republicans.

Supervising local campaign work.— Registration, doorbell-ringing, and election-day work can be handled only by local men on the sidewalks. A state organization can merely encourage and train them. PAC and the Democratic party were the only organizations which had extensive branches in counties, wards, and precincts in 1950. The party had some kind of organization in all eighty-eight counties. PAC had about eighty county and city subsidiaries, with ward and precinct organizations in a few of the larger communities. But, while the party branches operated practically autonomously, PAC could co-ordinate its fewer subdivisions fairly effectively.

One way of co-ordinating PAC subdivisions was the annual state convention. Although Taft was not specifically mentioned at the state CIO convention, the delegates agreed upon some basic political objectives for the state CIO. Another means of co-ordination was the state PAC committee of about one hundred members from local councils and unions. They met five or six times during the 1950 campaign to plan state-wide strategy and policy. The most effective co-ordination and supervision, however, came from PAC's state staff. On April 21 the staff organized an institute to train local PAC workers. They were responsible for the "kickoff" rally in Columbus, attended by three thousand delegates from all over the state. They passed information down to the lower echelons via the *Monthly Review* and innumerable personal letters. Most important, staff members were assigned to specific local areas to give direct personal supervision to campaign work.

Local PAC's were instructed to emphasize Ferguson above all other candidates. On the theory that "a large vote is a Democratic vote," they were encouraged to push registration and election-day work. Local PAC's, like that in Steubenville, got state funds for building their ward and precinct organizations. Separate international unions were whipped into action. The state passed its literature down through all these developing outlets.

The Democratic party had a larger and better-established local network than PAC. Its workers were not new to registration, precinct, and election-day work. Furthermore, their reward for party activity was often more tangible than the reward of PAC workers. But these local party subsidiaries were not so well co-ordinated as PAC, and they spent their efforts in behalf of county rather than state-wide candidates.

In summary, PAC had considerable influence on the conduct of Ferguson's campaign. This was not because it held an "inside track" with Ferguson or the party but simply because it campaigned so actively while other Democratic groups scarcely campaigned at all. In arousing itself politically, it did produce a good share of the money, publicity, and local activity that went into the campaign.

Advantages and Limitations of a Supplemental Relationship

Despite labor's efforts, Ferguson was decisively defeated. PAC was crestfallen. How effective was a supplemental relationship as a means of influencing the election process? What were its limitations?

PAC could point to some returns on its efforts. It had expanded its political organization, registered thousands of new voters, introduced many unionists to political action for the first time, and given its workers and leaders badly needed political experience. It had strengthened itself for future campaigns. But as a method of defeating Taft in 1950, a supplemental relationship had its drawbacks.

According to George Baldanzi, of the Textile Workers, one of its worst features was that PAC was left backing a second-rate candidate. Ferguson was not as able as Taft in campaigning, nor would he have operated so skilfully in the Senate. He did not catch the imagination of liberals the way Taft caught the imagination of conservatives. The best PAC could do was to tell its members that Ferguson was a "common man," evolving from "humble origins," and certainly better than Taft. From its supplemental position PAC could help in the campaign but not in the choice of candidates. To make this internal party decision PAC would have had to wave more votes at preprimary negotiations or at the primary itself.

The state PAC director mentioned a second vexing problem, when he said, "The Democratic party is a vacuum." The state party was a rather sad affair, unable to co-ordinate its subsidiaries and unwilling to back its own candidate. Party inactivity left PAC "holding the bag." Not only did labor have to provide most of Ferguson's resources, but it did not even operate under a friendly party "cover," as business groups operated under the Republican party. Lack of state party support was a serious handicap to Ferguson. As a supplemental group, however, PAC could not remedy the situation. A better campaign required a shift of power inside the party itself, and PAC was not operating at this internal level.

A third problem was described by Ferguson's publicity manager. "Labor," he said, "operates too much aboveboard." Taft made endless use of the idea that PAC had "captured" the Democratic party. When the voter saw quantities of Ferguson literature with a labor label, PAC workers ringing doorbells, and poll watchers with labor banners, he began to think Taft was right. Labor, on the other hand, felt it had to operate openly. Rounding up the vote of a million wokers required a dramatic appeal difficult to conceal from public view. Ferguson's campaign technique made the problem worse. By depending on interest groups to arouse their own members, he made active groups like PAC noticeable. After the campaign was over, Ferguson's publicity manager, Clarence Doyle, regretted this: "We now realize that workers are not reached just through their union organizations. They are also veterans, newspaper readers, and church members. Next time we will work out a general, rather than a segmental, appeal" (interview, November 15,

1950). PAC would not have left itself so exposed if it had entered the structure of the Democratic party.

PAC's exposure would not have been so bad if its public relations had been better. Many voters who found political activity by the Chamber of Commerce natural considered similar activity by labor practically subversive. Even some union members felt this way. To these voters the terms "labor," "socialism," and "communism" were vaguely related—degrees of something "un-American." When they witnessed the activity of PAC, they feared the revolution was under way. The commercial press did nothing to correct this impression. The only large papers to indorse Ferguson were the *Dayton News*, the *Springfield Sun*, and the *Lancaster Eagle Gazette*. Many papers like the *Youngstown Vindicator* were bitterly antilabor. Fear of socialism, vaguely defined, was reinforced by the extensive advertising of the NAM and the AMA. Even potentially compatible interest groups became afraid that combinations with PAC would be a "kiss of death." The problem was too fundamental for PAC to remedy with a few liaison officers. Such public attitudes were related to a tense international situation and to the considerable power of interest groups to whom PAC was anathema. PAC was living in a hostile world which it could not control. Faced with a similar problem, the Michigan PAC entered the Democratic party, where it could operate quietly under a label that did not arouse so much fear in the average voter.

Why Did PAC Supplement the Party in Ohio?

Armchair strategists may criticize: Why didn't PAC nominate a more acceptable candidate? Why didn't it enter the Democratic party? Why didn't it start a third party? Such strategists forget that party relationships are not built of wishful thoughts but of money in the chest and ballots in the box.

What political resources were necessary to establish internal or third-party relationships in Ohio in 1950? What resources did PAC have? These concrete problems may explain why PAC had to adopt a supplemental relationship, despite its limitations.

The election district.—In Michigan an interest group could control a state party convention by controlling the delegation of one large county. Fortunately for the Michigan PAC, its voters were concentrated in this same strategic county. But in Ohio no one county had sufficient Democratic votes to boss the state party. The two largest counties, Hamilton and Cuyahoga, together produced less than 29 per cent of Ohio's Democratic senatorial vote in 1946. Union members were also well scattered throughout the state. PAC would have had to control five or six large county parties in order to obtain a significant bloc of votes inside the Ohio State Democratic Committee. Since it did not have sufficient resources to capture these county parties in 1950, PAC remained outside the party.

Election practices.—PAC was handicapped by that section of the Taft-Hartley Act which forbids unions as well as corporations from making contributions directly from their treasuries to candidates for federal office. The provision may look just, but PAC felt it put labor at a disadvantage. PAC was forced to raise its funds by soliciting small voluntary contributions from thousands of individual members—a difficult task. Corporatons had fewer, but wealthier, contacts. Furthermore, corporations could still contribute directly to "better-business" groups like the Ohio Association of Manufacturers. This group, not being a corporation, could contribute directly to federal political campaigns, whereas PAC, regarded as a union, could not.

A second election practice posed a limitation on PAC's voting potential. All the larger cities of Ohio, where industrial workers and Democrats are concentrated, require registration for voting. Much of PAC's effort thus had to be expended on getting its members registered. Some election boards helped by making registration as easy as possible. Others did not. Because of the registration requirement, some of PAC's potential voters found themselves disqualified.

Compatible interest groups.—In 1950 the Ohio PAC did not have enough votes of its own to elect a candidate in the primaries, to enter the state level of the Democratic party, or to form a successful third party. But could it have formed a coalition of compatible interest groups with enough strength to maintain these more influential party relationships?

PAC is not the only labor federation. Ohio's 550,000 AF of L members, 150,000 mine, railway, and independent union members, plus its 500,000 CIO members, could be of tremendous political significance if active and united. In 1950 these groups did combine in the United Labor League. But this was a temporary committee united only for the defeat of Taft. The labor federations still indorsed their candidates separately; the federations were not equally active; and their political work was poorly co-ordinated at the community level. It is doubtful whether these labor groups could have agreed upon united internal or third-party political action, because traditional suspicions and rivalries still existed. Without unity, the forms of political action requiring great politcal resources were impossible.

Minority groupings, like Negroes, might have found themselves compatible with PAC. Ohio's Negro voters were not active politically, however, and they were not organized into strong interest groups. The Ohio Association for the Advancement of Colored People and the Urban League did not make political indorsements. The patronage groups which had strength among Negroes in some cities could scarcely have co-operated with PAC in internal or third-party activity. It proved difficult to establish a coalition with Negro groups for anything but supplemental activity.

In Michigan PAC formed a coalition with liberal intellectuals which was strong enough to wrest control of the Democratic party. But groups like the Americans for Democratic action in Ohio were small and skeptical of partisan activity. There was no agressive partisan organization among young liberals to compare with the Young Democrats of Michigan. PAC could not count on them for great resources for internal or third-party activity.

Liberal farmers suffered from the same difficulties as intellectual liberals. They were not organized into active political interest groups. Rural co-operatives were often hesitant to "get mixed up in politics." The Ohio Farm Bureau, though one of the most liberal in the country, refused to line up with PAC, even behind Murray Lincoln. In 1950, farm groups were a poor source of support for PAC maneuvers.

PAC might have tried a coalition with various patronage groups, but such arrangements were also unlikely in 1950. Many patronage politicians considered PAC's support a "kiss of death," and PAC, for its part, hesitated to get mixed up in "dirty politics." In most communities, as in Steubenville, PAC did not have enough votes to get control of local parties. It might have become merely a dissatisfied minority among stronger patronage interest groups if it had tried to enter the party.

Since the prospect of coalition was limited, PAC stuck to a supplemental position.

Voting behavior.—Judging from the Democratic primary vote in recent years, PAC would have needed between 110,000 and 160,000 votes to put its own candidate on the final Democratic ballot. Murray Lincoln, like PAC itself, estimated that labor could not produce this vote in 1950 and declined to run. Since it did not have enough votes for effective primary action itself, PAC had to be content to supplement anyone who happened to win the primary.

Was the Ohio PAC in a position to balance power in 1950 and thus bargain with both parties? Despite its considerable efforts, PAC would have needed 430,880 more votes than it had, to change the outcome of the election. Except for 1944, Republicans had elected senators by more than a 5 per cent margin since 1938. A balance of power required more resources than PAC possessed; its own vote was too small and the difference between the parties too great.

How about a third-party relationship? Judging from the past, a third party would need well over 1,000,000 votes to challenge Republican and Democratic contenders. This seemed conpletely out of the question in 1950 for a PAC which doubted if it could raise 160,000 votes in the primary. AF of L and most independent liberal groups were not enthusiastic about third parties. If it really wanted to defeat Taft, PAC's best chance was to back Ferguson.

Ohio PAC structure.—According to its *Rules of Operation,* state PAC policy is formulated by a state central committee of about one hundred members. This committee is composed of (1) officers of the Ohio CIO and members of the Ohio Executive Board; (2) one representative of each international union with members in Ohio, plus all international directors and CIO regional directors in Ohio; (3) chairmen of each county or city PAC; (4) chairmen of each congressional district PAC; and (5) a representative of the women's auxiliary. A good proportion of the state PAC is union staff personnel. During 1950 this full committee met five or six times to make final indorsements and approve campaign strategy. The real work of planning PAC policy was done by a steering committee of nineteen.

State PAC executive work in 1950 was performed by a staff of eight full-time state council workers. In addition to the state director and his assistant, this staff consisted of a publicity director, statistician, representative to minority groups, representative to farm and church groups, and representatives assigned to specific areas in the state. They were aided during the campaign by four national PAC staff workers and by full-time local workers in Cleveland, Cincinnati, Toledo, and Youngstown.

Since the state PAC was established in 1943, it has brought to life about eighty county and district PAC's throughout the state. Many of these were in the process of building independent ward and precinct organizations in 1950. In addition, the state PAC received support from political-action committees established at local, regional, and national levels of various separate international unions, such as the United Automobile Workers and the Textile Workers Union of America.

What is the division of authority within this PAC structure? The Ohio PAC had close ties with the national PAC. The national director, Jack Kroll, was president of the Ohio CIO Council and manager of an Amalgamated Clothing Workers' joint board in Cincinnati. The national office has not been enthusiastic about third-party or internal party activity, and this mood was reflected in the Ohio PAC decision to back a Democrat rather than run an independent.

Ohio's PAC was built from the state level down rather than from the local, city, and county level up. It has been directed largely by union staff rather than by rank-and-file union members. As a result, policy decisions have been made generally at the state level, while PAC's in the communities acted as executive arms. The centralization of authority made possible a high degree of co-ordination. County PAC's were not autonomous, as were county Democratic parties. But this same centralization restricted local experimentation with different methods of political action. All local groups subscribed to the same statement in the *Rules of Operation:* "It is our avowed and determined purpose to maintain political non-partisanship and independence of thought and function." This state PAC policy may have discouraged experimentation with internal (and therefore partisan) methods of political influence.

PAC's composition.—PAC's strength, like that of any group, depends, in the long run, on the energy and ability of the human beings who run it. What kind of political action were CIO leaders, workers, and members willing and prepared to undertake in 1950?

The ability and preferences of leaders play an important part in strategy decisions. Jack Kroll, president of the Ohio CIO Council and national director of PAC, had considerable political experience. Jacob Clayman, executive director of the Ohio State council, had less experience but was an able and hard-working executive. Both were sincerely concerned with achieving PAC's immediate political objectives, but neither advocated internal or third-party action in 1950. Their preference for supplemental action may have come from a realization of PAC's limited resources or from an aversion to the compromises which would have been necessary for partisan activity; or they may have felt more at home in supplemental political action. In any case, their preferences had great influence on PAC's decision to back Ferguson in 1950.

Lack of experienced secondary leaders and workers in Ohio's districts and precincts was one of PAC's serious limitations. In most areas PAC district and county leaders could not compare in political experience or connections with local party leaders.

PAC's precinct workers were concentrated in a few localities and often were undertaking this difficult job for the first time. Party groups, on the other hand, had precinct workers throughout the state, frequently with considerable political experience. PAC just did not have enough trained political workers to accept the responsibility of controlling an old party or creating a new one.

The success or failure of any party relationship rests, in the end, on the convictions of rank-and-file union members. Do they feel strongly enough about the issues involved to register and vote according to PAC's indorsement? Conviction determines the size of voting resources, which, in turn, determines the party relationship that PAC can afford. The average Ohio CIO member was not so distressed about PAC's issues as to become extremely active in pushing them in 1950. He lived in the same political environment as his nonunion neighbors. He was often subject to their vague fear of "communism," with no precise definition of that term. He had his suspicions about all authorities, whether they were factory "bosses," political "bosses," or labor "bosses." After seeing his local party machine in action, politics looked like "dirty business" to him. He may have favored CIO's legislative demands; he may have preferred Ferguson to Taft; but he still looked upon his union as an economic rather than a political weapon. He did not see the labor movement as a political crusade in which his personal interests were deeply involved. As a result of this rank-and-file inertia, PAC had to bestir itself considerably to get CIO members registered and out to vote. It had hoped that 80 per cent of the 500,000 CIO members in Ohio would register and that 8½ out of 10 would vote for Ferguson. November returns indicated that about 70 per cent had voted and that 7 out of 10 had voted Democratic. This amounted to about 245,000 CIO votes which followed PAC's indorsement. But many of these unionists would have voted Democratic anyway, and the same vote could not be counted upon for internal or third-party action. The actual concern of CIO members thus sets narrow limits to the influence of PAC and the relationship it can establish with the parties.

Summary

In Ohio in 1950, PAC did not make an indorsement in the primary, enter the Democratic party, or start a third party. It simply supplemented Ferguson's campaign by organizing CIO members in his behalf. It performed this task, however, with considerably more gusto than the Democratic party or other interest groups. So, while it had little influence on internal party decisions, it did leave its imprint on the campaign.

This supplemental relationship had limitations as a means for achieving PAC's legislative objectives. PAC was left backing a candidate whom it did not really admire. It received almost no support from a weak and hostile state Democratic party, and it was exposed to public view as a "radical" special-interest group. But PAC did not have the political resources necessary for more influential activity. Its rank-and-file members were incompletely activated. Its workers and leaders were inexperienced. Its finances were limited by the Taft-Hartley Act and the problems of fund-raising. As if this were not enough, effective political action in Ohio required a particularly great outlay of resources. PAC could get relatively little help from potentially compatible interest groups because of their suspicions and lack of organization. The major parties could not be balanced easily because Republican senatorial candidates had substantial majorities. Entering the party with a share of control was difficult because county machines were strong and Ohio's electoral configuration unfavorable. PAC was almost forced to supplement any Democrat if it hoped to see Taft defeated.

III *Steubenville: PAC Balances Power*

THE Eighteenth Congressional District of Ohio (see Fig. 1) is composed of five counties lying along the Ohio River on the eastern border of the state. Most of the people in this area are farmers or miners, though a few work in the pottery plants in Columbiana County. The only city of any size is Steubenville, a smoky, steel-producing community in Jefferson County.

This district was strongly Republican until the depression, when it became equally strongly Democratic. Since the passing of the New Deal era, however, the district has fluctuated between Republicans and Democrats. In Jefferson County, where this story occurs, both parties have strong machines and elections often run close. In 1950 the Eighteenth District re-elected its liberal Democratic Congressman, Wayne Hays, contrary to the Republican trend in most of Ohio. The state CIO thought that its Eighteenth District PAC had a lot to do with this. The Democratic party claimed that victory was due largely to its energetic young chairman in Jefferson County. This chapter is a study of the relationship between the Eighteenth District PAC and the Jefferson County Democratic party at the time of their common campaign to return Wayne Hays to Congress. It illustrates the case of a PAC which supplemented a Democratic candidate and had enough votes to swing the county in a close election.

EIGHTEENTH
CONGRESSIONAL DISTRICT
OF OHIO

Fig. 1

PAC and the Jefferson County Democratic Party

Three political structures actively backed Hays in Jefferson County in 1950: the county Democratic party, the Hays for Congress Committee, and PAC. How did PAC relate itself to the structure of the other two organizations?

Jefferson County elects 130 Democratic precinct captains at its primaries every other year. About a fortnight after their election these captains meet as the Central Democratic Committee to elect their county party chairman. This is their one and only responsibility. After the decision is made, the committee dies, and the chairman takes over. He picks an executive committee of 55 or 60 members, representatives of party groups which he needs or trusts. But this unwieldy executive committee has little more life than the county committee. It meets three or four times a year, merely to ratify the chairman's decision. The chairman is virtual party dictator, once elected. He makes the real decisions about candidates, discipline, organization, and patronage, practically single-handed. This party organization is the perfect basis for a machine. The chairman's power can be challenged only by electing sufficient precinct captains to depose him at the biennial county committee meeting.

PAC did not deliberately run precinct delegates for the county committee in the 1950 primaries, although 10 or 12 of the 130 precinct captains elected happened to be CIO members, running as individuals. The chairman appointed 4 or 5 union men to his executive committee, but only 2 of these were active PAC members. One was secretary-treasurer of Local 1190 Steelworkers' PAC. He acted as liaison between the party and the interest group, reporting on party activity to PAC and acting as PAC's contact with the party chairman. But, since PAC had only 2 sure votes out of 58 on an executive committee which had little power anyway, it was hardly in a position to exert much internal party influence.

The Jefferson Democratic party has built an organization out in the wards and precincts. This present organization is directed by the county chairman and is composed of the 130 elected precinct captains, 49 of whom come from the six wards of the county's largest city, Steubenville. Most of these precinct workers are active only at campaign time, however, when they contact and register Democratic voters and watch the polls. The chairman pays active workers by patronage or a small fee on election day. Instead of entering this Democratic precinct organization, PAC organized its own ward and precinct structure. With this independent setup, it could swing its vote easily from party to party. For its precinct organization PAC divides Jefferson County into two PAC areas, each with an area chairman. At campaign time each of these chairmen finds PAC workers for the precincts in his area. Each worker is expected to contact and register all CIO members in his neighborhood, to distribute literature, and to watch the polls. Like party workers, active PAC workers often receive a small remuneration for election-day work.

In 1950 PAC and the party happened to support the same congressional candidate, Wayne Hays. Therefore, their precinct workers co-operated, exchanging literature and using the same cars. After contacting CIO members, PAC workers transported Democrats to the polls on election day. Every effort was made, nevertheless, to keep party and PAC precinct organizations separate. PAC and the party compared lists to see that no worker doubled his pay by acting as a party worker and a PAC worker at the same time. This was more than an economy measure, however. In the next election PAC workers might well be supporting a Republican candidate for mayor.

A third political organization at work for Hays in 1950 was the Hays for Congress Committee. As a cattle-raiser and Belmont County commissioner, Hays had good contacts of his own with rural and Democratic groups. These contacts became the nucleus of his personal campaign committee. The committee took care of Hays's personal publicity, while PAC and the party provided precinct workers. PAC was not represented on Hays's committee, but Hays co-ordinated PAC work with his own by close personal contact.

In Jefferson County, therefore, PAC did not attempt to enter the Democratic party or the candidate's committee. Instead, it established its own ward and precinct organization quite independently of the party and acted as an independent external interest group.

PAC and Internal Party Decisions

The Eighteenth District PAC, like the state PAC, had almost no direct voice on internal party councils. But, in Jefferson County, PAC could do some indirect talking because it had a bloc of votes which the party needed very badly in winning the election. The Democratic chairman admitted that the indorsement of Local 1190's PAC probably won the election for Steubenville's Republican mayor in 1949. In 1950 the difference between Hays and his Republican opponent in Jefferson County was only 575 votes. Without PAC's vote, small as it may have been, Hays might well have lost the county. It was merely political sanity for the Democratic chairman to take labor's vote into account when making party decisions. PAC had bargaining power because of its balancing position.

Selecting a candidate.—Hays was not from Jefferson County. In fact, he was defeated in the Jefferson primary of 1948, though he won in the rest of the congressional district. In 1950, however, Hugo Alexander, a powerful local politician, then fighting for the party chairmanship, gave Hays his tacit support, even though he was not a "local boy." Alexander was satisfied with Hays because his voting record had not alienated potential Democrtic groups like labor and because his patronage disbursements had pleased the party. With Alexander's tacit support, Hays won the 1950 county primary by a large majority.

PAC helped Hays's nomination in a more official, though probably less significant, way. On February 21, PAC sent letters to the two Democratic and three Republican primary contenders, asking them to appear before its interviewing committee. Some of the candidates appeared in person and were questioned on legislation of interest to CIO. On March 14 the district PAC indorsed Hays for the primary, because of "his liberal voting record and position as incumbent Congressman." It thereupon gave him publicity at union meetings and in union papers.

PAC thus helped Hays's nomination in two ways. Its official indorsement probably netted him some votes, and Alexander was thinking of labor's vote when he gave Hays the nod.

Electing party officers.—The only important party officer in Jefferson County is the county chairman. Once elected, he gives the final word on party decisions. Various patronage groups have disputed over this party position since 1944, when "Jackie" Nolan, colorful founder and "boss" of the county machine, was scalded to death in his shower. Nolan's son willed the job to Hawthorn, a weak politician, when he left for the Marines in 1946, but the Irish contingent under Slee defeated Hawthorn in 1948. In 1950 Alexander negotiated a few clever "deals" and seized the crown.

Alexander was an able and energetic young lawyer with

patronage objectives. He had learned the rudiments of politics, patronage, protection, and human nature from eight years as "Boss" Nolan's prosecuting attorney. He was acceptable to various interest groups. Steubenville thought of him as its "home-town boy." CIO considered him "one of the boys" because he had once worked in the steel mills. To Italians he was a "paisan." The Chamber of Commerce respected him as the owner of several businesses. Various patronage and protection-oriented groups were said to feel obligated to him. Reformers and Republicans claimed he played "dirty politics" but admitted that he had a way with the interest groups. The town generally agreed he was "Jackie" Nolan's logical heir.

PAC did not dispute Alexander's election by trying to run its precinct captains against his. On the contrary, PAC has felt quite satisfied with this "friendly" party chairman.

Expanding party organization.—Upon his election, Alexander lost no time in rebuilding the party organization. He strengthened his ward and precinct structure by encouraging year-round precinct work. Though labor and minority groups were better organized and more demanding than in Nolan's day, Alexander drew on their support by a judicious distribution of patronage and candidates. Labor has condoned Alexander's expanding Democratic organization by indorsing its candidates. But PAC did not help build this structure. It spent its resources developing its own independent bases in the wards and precincts.

Disciplining party interest groups.—While Alexander had the authority to distribute party spoils, he had to keep in mind the groups from whom he hoped to receive support, and his restless supporters were not easily satisfied.

In its balancing position PAC could hardly be considered a "faithful" party supporter, but its demands were to be kept in mind, nevertheless. PAC could not only deny its votes to the Democrats but swing them to the Republicans. Actually, PAC did not express much interest in routine patronage jobs. Its members were more securely and profitably employed in the steel mills. PAC intimated that it might be interested in placing hardship cases and strikers, but this problem did not arise in 1950. PAC expressed definite interest, however, in certain local policy-making jobs. It wanted a voice in determining who should head local relief, housing, and civilian-defense programs. PAC wanted sympathetic local justices when it came to settling injunction disputes. Local 1190 PAC in Steubenville showed little hesitancy in proposing names for such jobs. And it was in a position to demand some, though not overriding, consideration from the party chairman and congressman.

In summary, PAC could exert more pressure on internal party decisions from its balancing position in Steubenville than from its supplementary position in the state. Since its votes were crucial in a final election, it had a say in selecting candidates and distributing patronage.

PAC in Hays's Campaign

PAC, the Hays committee, and the county Democratic party all campaigned vigorously for Hays. How active was PAC compared to these other groups? What influence did it have on the conduct of the campaign?

Fund-raising.—It is impossible to decipher how much PAC and the Democratic party spent in electing Hays in Jefferson County. Both organizations supported a whole slate rather than a single candidate, and PAC's contribution was spread throughout the entire congressional district. A rough comparison can be drawn, nevertheless.

The Jefferson County party gave Hays no direct financial

assistance. But it did supply him, along with the other candidates on the Democratic ticket, with rallies, banquets, sample ballots, and precinct and election-day workers. A party executive committee member estimates that the county party spent about $20,000 for its entire ticket in the 1950 campaign. The Hays for Congress Committee purchased most of Hays's personal publicity. It spent $3,000 on Hays in the Eighteenth District, $2,200 of which came from the Democratic National Committee and $800 from Hays's personal friends.

PAC spent $5,258.14 in the Eighteenth District. One thousand dollars of this came from the Ohio state PAC, $500 from the national PAC, $829.44 from voluntary contributions, and $2,928.70 from a monthly per capita tax on locals. PAC spent this money for its entire slate, however, and Ferguson, rather than Hays, got first priority. Hays received about $700 of this, plus the benefit of PAC's precinct work. PAC spent most of its money itself, buying literature and hiring precinct workers. Only $600 was given directly to county Democratic parties. Hays received no cash. Alexander estimated that PAC provided only about one-tenth of the total funds spent for Hays in Jefferson County. As a result, the community thought of Hays as a Democratic, rather than a labor, candidate. PAC's money did not greatly influence the general conduct of the campaign, but it did strengthen PAC's independent precinct structure and increase the size of its own voting bloc.

Registration.—Steubenville is the only community in Jefferson County requiring registration. In the 1950 campaign the Republican and Democratic parties, the Junior Chamber of Commerce, PAC, and the newspapers bestirred themselves to get voters qualified. The Democratic patry conducted its drive through precinct captains and ten or fifteen hired workers. Precinct workers reported unregistered Democrats to party headquarters, and registration workers contacted potential voters personally.

PAC worked intensively on Stenbenville's 5,500 CIO members. Local 1190 checked its membership list with the election board and sent a reminder to every unregistered member. It actually transported 135 of its 600 unregistered members to the election board. By the October deadline, 80 per cent of its members were registered. Since PAC limited its drive to its own membership, it increased its own political resources but did not have a spectacular influence on total registration. Registration in Steubenville in 1950 was only 138 above the 1948 registration.

Publicity.—The Hays for Congress Committee took care of most of Hays's personal publicity: cards, matches, campaign cars, fair booths, and radio and newspaper announcements. Hays says his committee distributed 300,000 pieces of literature throughout the district, 60,000 in Jefferson County alone. He spoke before a variety of groups, including labor.

Democratic party publicity supported the entire slate, though it did not display PAC's enthusiasm for Mr. Ferguson. A thousand people attended the party "kickoff" dance at a Steubenville night club. Party headquarters produced an inexpensive luncheon once a week, open to anyone and followed by Bingo for the ladies. The Jefferson party also sponsored radio programs and contributed $500 worth of newspaper advertising to Hays. Hays also shared the benefit of the contacts of party precinct workers and of the Democratic sample ballot. The party did not produce much literature itself. It handled a few of PAC's pieces, but the chairman expressed little enthusiasm for it because of its limited appeal.

Chief credit for literature must go to PAC, which placed three-quarters of a million pieces for its slate throughout the

entire district. Most of this flood came from the state PAC office and included candidate's records, special bulletins for Negro and farm groups, and thousands of Taft comic books. The
district PAC also distributed a few of its own pieces and sample
ballots. Local PAC's used their news letters. Some of this literature was mailed directly to CIO members, and school children
and PAC workers carried the remainder from door to door. In
one community, when citizens opened their Republican newspaper one evening, out fell the anti-Taft comic book. Needless
to say, the newspaper deplored this method of distribution!
PAC publicity was styled for its own members and looked
somewhat extreme to nonunion eyes. PAC relied on quantities
of this colorful publicity rather than on quiet personal arrangements with other interest groups. The effect, as with Ferguson,
was to expose PAC to Republican war cries.

Interest-group contacts.—The strong party chairmen of Jefferson County have been masters of the process of arousing
interest groups and combining their resources. Alexander did
something labor could not do for itself: he brought Mine
Workers, AF of L, CIO, and county party leaders together
four or five times to integrate their publicity and election-day
work.

According to its by-laws, the Eighteenth District PAC is
composed of representatives of any organization "which will
concur in the policies of CIO regarding political action"; but,
actually, PAC has not been adept at consolidating interest
groups. The local AF of L was not active politically. It sent
two unofficial representatives to PAC but never formally affiliated. The railway lodges sent no one. The United Mine Workers campaigned actively for Hays but not in coordination with
PAC. Aside from a few pieces of campaign literature, PAC
made little effort to activate Negro groups. The state PAC sent

its representative to conduct a discussion group between industrial workers and farmers, but this was scarcely a serious attempt to come to terms with powerful farm groups. Hays would not let labor campaign for him in rural areas, where he figured the PAC label would be a liability. The party rather than the PAC thus reaped the electoral fruits of reconciling interest groups.

Election-day work.—Alexander, the Democratic chairman, placed party workers in all 130 county precincts on both primary and general election days and paid them ten dollars a day for their services.

PAC angered the party by paying its workers twelve dollars. It turned out 30 or 40 PAC workers for the primary and 127 on general election day. At the suggestion of the party chairman, PAC did not distribute its workers evenly among precincts but concentrated them where CIO members lived.

Steubenville had no particular problem with election fraud. PAC and party workers spent most of their time checking voters and fetching their own supporters. PAC was the only group which helped the party perform this function. In doing so, however, it undoubtedly added to its own voting bloc.

Advantages and Limitations of a Balance of Power

The Eighteenth Congressional District PAC had more influence on the party than did the Ohio PAC. Because PAC had a crucial vote, the party chairman was "friendly." He had good cause to remember PAC when it came to supporting candidates and distributing patronage. Because the party campaigned actively, Hays could not be damned as labor's candidate, and PAC could not be accused of "capturing" the party.

But this balance-of-power relationship also had its limitations. While PAC could wrest certain concessions from the party, it had no direct voice in making party decisions. Alexander, as party chairman, might well have given his approval to a conservative rather than a liberal candidate if he had felt this would increase the party vote. If he decided to solicit the support of the syndicates or Ohio Association of Manufacturers, PAC could show its displeasure only by shifting its vote. Alexander would undoubtedly treat PAC as he had treated Slee, if PAC attempted to "capture" party control. Alexander was a pragmatic patronage-oriented politician. To him PAC's issues were a means to power. To make its issues the real goal of the party, PAC would have had to capture the chairmanship for itself.

In the second place, the Republicans did not bargain actively for labor's vote. Though Republican candidates appeared before PAC indorsement committees and recognized labor's balancing position, they could not afford to make many concessions. By giving in on Taft-Hartley, for example, they would have lost more from business interests than they gained from labor. The lack of competition between parties for PAC's vote reduced labor's bargaining power.

A third problem which a balance of power presented to PAC was training union members to be independent voters. CIO members were asked to vote Democratic in one election and Republican in the next, or even to split their ballot in the same election. This necessitated far more political education than did straight party voting. Such independence was roundly denounced by regular party workers. CIO members, like many other Americans, had traditional party loyalties which were difficult to break. PAC could overcome this difficulty only by wider political education or by adopting a partisan party relationship.

Hays did not suffer from his labor connections as severely

as Ferguson, because the Hays committee and the Democratic party overshadowed PAC in activity and the local paper did not specifically victimize the local PAC. Nevertheless, many Steubenville citizens had not yet accepted PAC as a "respectable" interest group. The *Steubenville Herald Star* faithfully carried Taft's pronouncements about Communist influence in the CIO. Hays would not let PAC campaign openly for him outside Steubenville. PAC had a public relations problem which could be solved only by more effort to make itself acceptable to other community groups or by operating quietly under a respectable cover.

And, finally, a balance of power is a very perishable commodity. PAC's few hundred votes might be crucial when parties were evenly divided, as in 1950, but they might prove absolutely insignificant in a Republican landslide in 1952. By 1952 Alexander might have built a machine strong enough to win without PAC support. PAC's influence rested on a chance occurrence which it could not itself control—a close balance between the major parties.

Why Did PAC Balance Power in Jefferson County?

Though a balance-of-power relationship was more influential than a supplemental relationship, it still presented limitations. But it was probably the most influential relationship that PAC could afford, in view of its slender resources and the difficulty of "capturing" old parties or founding new ones in Jefferson County.

The election district.—In order to elect a party chairman, PAC would probably need the support of 66 of the 130 precinct captains in Jefferson County. But CIO's membership was concentrated in Steubenville Wards 1 to 3 and in Mingo Junction. These areas had a total of only 23 precincts. It is doubtful whether PAC could have found, much less elected, precinct captains in parts of Wards 5 and 6 or in rural areas. PAC's votes were not distributed over enough precincts to enable it to elect a majority of precinct captains to the county committee.

Compatible interest groups.—Could PAC have pooled its resources with other compatible interest groups to capture a party or create a new party?

Jefferson County boasted of 6,500 CIO members, 800 AF of L members, a small lodge of Railway Trainmen, and 3,000 Mine Workers. This bloc of votes could have done a lot if active and united. Actually, however, the Trainmen conducted almost no political activity, and the Mine Workers, though active, showed no inclination to work with CIO. The Democratic party chairman was able to get labor groups to cooperate more readily than PAC could. They were thus scarcely a promising nucleus for internal or third-party activity.

In order to elect a majority of precinct captains or attempt a serious third party, PAC would need at least some support from rural precincts. The chief organized interest groups among Jefferson County farmers were the Farm Bureau and the Grange, neither of which wasted any love on PAC. According to Hays, the PAC label was a liability in rural communities.

Steubenville is perhaps undeservedly famous for another interest group, its gambling and vice syndicates, which have displayed considerable skill in influencing both parties. They have also shown remarkable rapport with other interest groups in the community. After a night-club murder in 1947, twelve of Steubenville's ministers organized an antivice crusade, which brought some of these connections to light. In a blaze of publicity, the ministers called the local constabulary to act. Nothing happened. The mayor calmly asked the ministers to prove that there were houses of prostitution in Steubenville. Thereupon, the clergy asked to be deputized themselves. Republican and Democratic council members, including PAC representatives, voted solidly against "pistol-packing parsons." The Catholic bishop issued a public letter condemning the Protestant crusade: "We are against any attempt to make a major moral issue out of some moral fragment or even counterfeit morality. We do not intend to be swayed by false or erroneous consciences. . . . Gambling, considered in itself, is not wrong or sinful. . . . Drinking in itself is not evil (N. E. Nyguard, *Twelve against the Underworld* [New York: Hobson Book Press, 1947], p. 101)." Business groups also hesitated to join the crusade, claiming that a scandal would keep new industries out of Steubenville. Before long, even the Protestant churces lost enthusiasm. Some of their own members were said to own "redlight" property. The most active crusader left his church "at the request of his congregation." Gambling and vice interests, closed during the uproar, soon began operating again through smaller outlets more difficult to control. Evidently a number of interest groups found it better, in pursuing their own objectives, to have the financial resources of the syndicates with them rather than against them. In return, they offered to extend or condone protection. PAC in Steubenville started no crusades. Moral reform was not among its objectives. But, while PAC did not incur the wrath of the syndicates, neither did it get their support. Syndicates spent their funds pragmatically on the groups which actually held political control and were thus in a position to extend protection.

Could PAC expect support from Steubenville's nationality and racial groupings? The Italian community, of about three thousand members, was probably the best organized politically. It already had a political interest group with a patronage outlook, the American-Italian Democratic Club. This group was not a good partner, however, for internal or third-party moves by PAC. It was one of Chairman Alexander's mainstays. The Slavic community, with about two thousand voters, had a Polish-American Political Club, also patronage-oriented. In a moment of sharp disaffection, this group might combine with PAC to elect a party chairman, but in 1950 Alexander succeeded in keeping them well in line. In addition, Steubenville had over three thousand Negro voters. Though they might well have supported PAC's issues, they were not organized for political action. PAC would have had to organize them as Nolan had once organized Italian immigrants, in order to make them a tangible political resource.

Noticeable tension existed between Catholic and Protestant churches in Steubenville. With the ordination of an aggressive young bishop, Steubenville had become a Catholic center with five parochial grammar schools, a Catholic high school, and the city's only college. Protestant groups were disturbed. But religious competition took the form of a struggle for the consciences of the community rather than for its government. Close connection with either church might have split PAC's vote. It did well to "keep religion out of politics."

Thus PAC found difficulty in making coalitions. Compatible groups were not numerous, and the party chairman had been courting them for years.

Voting behavior.—Judging from the last three elections, PAC could swing a balance of power in county congressional elections by controlling from 300 to 3,000 votes. Electing a candidate of its own in the primary would have required from 3,000 to 5,000 votes. Entering the Democratic party with a chance to elect the county chairman would have required electing precinct captains carrying a primary vote of 3,000 to 4,000. A serious third party would have had to have an independent vote well over 16,000. Thus, unless election trends were to change suddenly or PAC were able to make combinations with other groups, the most effective relationship possible with 6,500 incompletely activated CIO members was a balance of power in close contests between major parties.

The Democratic party.—The particular structure, composition, and activity of the Jefferson County Democratic party made it difficult for insurgent groups to capture and difficult for a third party to defeat.

The Jefferson party did not have several important offices which members of an insurgent coalition could share. Control rested in the hands of one man, the chairman. In order to obtain control of the party, an interest group would have to elect the county chairman. This would be a difficult task, requiring money, votes, and careful organization in the precincts.

In 1950 the chairman of this county party was "friendly" to PAC. He was willing to grant concessions, especially on candidates, to win the labor vote. Thus PAC had little incentive to fight him.

In 1950 the party chairman had factionalism within the party under control. Italian and Polish groups were content to assent to his rule so long as they received patronage. There was therefore little internal party dissension which PAC could use in an internal bid for power.

And, finally, PAC was not caught with an inactive party organization, as at the state level. The Jefferson Democratic party was actively manning and expanding its organization and was producing and pushing its candidates. This internal strength made the party difficult to capture from inside or defeat from outside.

PAC's objectives.—If PAC had taken reform as one of its

objectives, it might have been unable to give even external support to the Jefferson County party, with its "questionable" relationship to the syndicates. If PAC's object had included control of the party, it would inevitably have faced a "showdown" with party ruler Alexander. If PAC had been primarily concerned with patronage, it might not have been able to work harmoniously with Italian and Polish groups. Internal or third-party activity would have been necessary to reach any of these goals.

But these were not the objectives of the Eighteenth District PAC in 1950. PAC was concerned primarily with the selection and election of a congressman committed to certain immediate legislative issues. In 1950 this limited goal could be reached fairly well by an external balance-of-power relationship with the county Democratic party.

PAC structure.—In the early 1940's, the CIO unions of Jefferson and two neighboring counties set up an industrial union council with a political-action arm. But the council was rent by "left wing"–"right wing" controversies and by factions concerned with local personalities and issues. These could not be reconciled, and the council collapsed.

In 1944, with some prodding from the state PAC, a political-action committee was established for the entire Eighteenth District. It was not attached to any CIO council. Instead, it was under the direct supervision of the state PAC. The district PAC confined its efforts to candidates for state and federal offices, since legislative standards for such candidates were defined at state and national CIO conventions. It thus avoided the factional strife involved in local indorsements, where issues are more confused and personalities more prominent.

Local PAC's in the Eighteenth District are free to dabble in local politics, however. The PAC of Wheeling steel's Local

1190 has been active in Steubenville and Jefferson County politics since 1942. It operates autonomously and has been able to elect representatives to the city council.

Thirty CIO locals have affiliated with the Eighteenth Congressional District PAC. Although each has one vote, representatives of only five or six attended 1950 PAC meetings regularly. Since five staff members also attended, staff personnel formed an important part of the committee.

District PAC meetings were not completely rubber-stamp affairs. Agenda included election of officers, preliminary indorsements, reports on local political activity, decisions on campaign finance, and co-ordination of campaign publicity and activity. But these were items of political execution rather than of policy-making. Final decisions on issues, strategy, and indorsements were made at the state level. The district PAC, unlike Local 1190 PAC, was primarily an executive arm. Rank-and-file interest and participation were not so great in the district as in the more or less autonomous local PAC. Contrary to the district, the local PAC was built from the bottom up and had policy-making power over local issues and strategy.

Composition of PAC.—The district PAC chairman in 1950 was John Rooney, assistant director of the state PAC. Since he lived and worked in Columbus rather than in Steubenville, he did not have the immediate contacts with community interest groups and CIO members necessary to enable him to build up a personal challenge to a party leader like Alexander. A staff member of the Steelworkers' regional office in Steubenville carried on PAC executive work in his absence. During the campaign this staff worker spent most of his time on PAC work. He worked hard, but he had neither the experience nor the inclination to run for the party chairmanship or to direct a third-party movement in the district. PAC's leaders were thus completely unprepared for internal or third-party activity.

The leaders of Local 1190 PAC had been active in Steubenville politics for several years. Two were on the Democratic Executive Committee. One ran for mayor on the Republican ticket. Another was a leader of the Young Republican Club. Several had served on the city council. None displayed any particular enthusiasm or capacity for the Democratic chairmanship or the leadership of a third party. They were practical politicians rather than crusaders.

In the bitter days of the depression, rank-and-file steelworkers were sufficiently concerned about their economic plight to join a union. In 1950, however, the average steelworker in Steubenville did not feel so concerned about political issues as to participate actively in PAC. It took some effort to get him registered, and it was no foregone conclusion, even then, that he would vote with PAC. On the basis of this membership interest, it would have been difficult to get enough rank-and-file support to build a successful third party or elect a Democratic party chairman.

One common attitude among rank-and-file union members favored the development of PAC's independent political organization, however. Many CIO members, like other Steubenville citizens, associated the regular party machines with "dirty politics." By pointing to its independence of both parties, PAC precinct workers were able to tap the support of both disillusioned Republicans and Democrats. If it had entered either party, PAC would have been tainted with their reputation.

Because of these limitations set by the community, the party, and labor itself in 1950, the best PAC could hope for in Jefferson County was a close election in which it could swing a balance of power.

Summary

The Eighteenth District PAC did not enter Democratic party structure. Instead, it built an independent ward and precinct organization among CIO members. With this it hoped to develop a loyal bloc of votes which it could offer to whichever candidate came closest to its demands.

Fortunately for PAC, the race between Republican and Democratic candidates was so close in some years that Democrats at least were willing to grant concessions to obtain labor's independent vote. For this reason the party chairman was friendly. He thought of labor when backing candidates and distributing jobs. He was willing to integrate labor's campaign with his own. PAC, for its part, felt little incentive to challenge the chairman's position.

While more satisfactory to PAC than a supplemental relationship, a balance of power presented limitations. PAC might demand concessions, but it could expect no share of control over party decisions. Republicans did not seriously compete for PAC's vote. It was difficult to get CIO members to drop their traditional party loyalties and become independent voters. Its independent precinct organization still left PAC exposed to the gaze of a hostile community. And, finally, PAC's balance of power would last only so long as the two major parties remained fairly equal in strength. A more influential relationship seemed unrealistic in Steubenville in 1950, however, because PAC's resources were too small and the party machine was too strong; PAC could not elect sufficient precinct captains to depose the party chairman; and it did not have enough votes to defeat a major party. A balance of power seemed to be the most feasible alternative.

IV   Chicago: PAC Fights
a Machine

THE Fifth Senatorial District of Illinois lies right in the heart
of Chicago. Cottage Grove Avenue divides it into two start-
lingly different worlds. On the eastern side is the University of
Chicago, a group of lake-shore hotels, and a middle-income
professional white community. On the western side is Bronze-
ville, Chicago's overcrowded Negro community, most of
whose inhabitants work at lower-paying industrial and service
trades.

The white community has a substantial Republican vote. In
1950 it elected a Republican congressman. But it also has an
active minority of liberal intellectuals, who tend to vote Democratic. The western side of Cottage Grove Avenue has shown
Democratic inclinations since the New Deal. For some time it
has returned William Dawson, a Negro Democrat, as its congressman. Both parties have strong machines in the Fifth Senatorial District. These machines are controlled by patronage
interest groups which show no particular sympathy toward
labor. The CIO, whose membership is largely in the Negro
community, formed an active independent PAC organization
in 1948. But how was this organization to make itself felt? The
alternatives were not easy. PAC decided to challenge the Democratic machine head-on at a primary. This is a study of the
relationship between the First Congressional District PAC and

five wards of the Cook County Democratic party as they grappled over the state senatorial nomination in the 1950 primary.

PAC and the Democratic Machine

Democratic party functions in the Fifth Senatorial District are directed by the leaders of the Third, Fourth, Fifth, Sixth, and Twentieth wards of Cook County, which lie at least partly within the boundaries of the district. PAC's political-action work is the responsibility of the First Congressional District PAC, whose jurisdiction covers about half the Fifth Senatorial District (see Fig. 2). What was the relationship between these two structures in 1950?

Chicago party ward leaders are elected every four years at primaries. Within their wards and within the limits set by the county chairman, they are "little bosses." They decide on the party's regular candidates for the primary, appoint and direct party precinct captains, discipline their followers, distribute party rewards, and direct campaigns. Internal rebellions, especially as a result of personality conflicts, have been known at the ward level. Sometimes these result in a primary battle, and, upon rare occasion, victory for the rebel. The First District PAC has never tried to enter party structure by electing such a ward leader.

The ward leader appoints at least one captain for each of the precincts in his ward. These precinct captains do the political legwork. They register voters, raise money, ring doorbells, call precinct meetings, and watch the polls in their neighborhoods. But they are only "errand boys." Since they are appointed, not elected, they do not make party decisions. They do not even vote for the county party leader, as in Steubenville. PAC would gain little by getting its members appointed as party precinct captains.

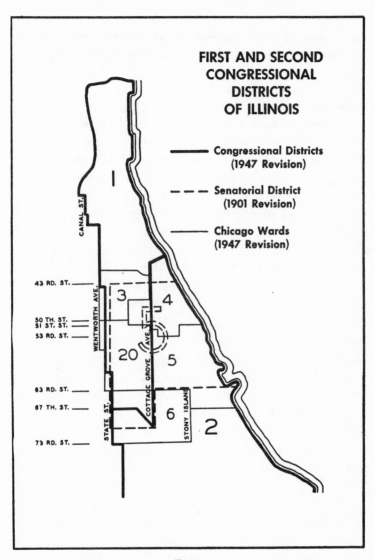

FIG. 2

Though they are elected at primaries and are responsible for party functions, Chicago ward leaders themselves are hardly free agents. The party leader can crack the big whip of patronage close to their ears. In 1950, for example, Chairman Jacob Arvey effectively removed Joseph Plunkett as Fourth Ward leader by channeling patronage through a more trustworthy committee. Actually, therefore, PAC could not raise its voice too high even by electing ward leaders. Control rests firmly in the hands of the county chairman, and PAC's chance of selecting this gentleman in 1950 was exceedingly remote.

Since it seemed impossible to enter the party with any control, PAC built its own independent organization right down through the wards and precincts. This First Congressional District PAC was one of the most active in Illinois. It was first organized in 1948 by Willoughby Abner, a regional political-action director for the United Automobile Workers. By 1950 he had established permanent headquarters on Forty-seventh Street, with offices, hall, and bar. He divided that section of the First Congressional District lying in the Fifth Senatorial District into thirty-two PAC areas and designated a leader for each. In the 1950 campaign these area leaders were able to locate 212 workers for the 361 precincts. This PAC organization attempted to produce the same internal and campaign functions as the party, though restricting its efforts mainly to CIO members and their families. By 1950 it felt strong enough to take on the party at a primary election.

PAC and Internal Party Decisions

With its independent political organization, what pressure could PAC bring to bear on internal party decisions?

Selecting a Democratic candidate.—Anyone who can submit

a bona fide petition can run in Cook County Democratic primaries, but that candidate who has the support of the party machine and is therefore known as the party regular is at a great advantage. The party's precinct organization is at his service. Primary election management and policing work to his advantage. The party faithful are more likely to show up on primary election day than "independents."

PAC tried, but failed to have any say about the party's regular candidate for state senator in 1950. Barnet Hodes, the Fifth Ward Democratic leader, claims he began the search for the regular candidate by appointing a committee of "responsible" Democrats. This committee included party, business, civic, and religous leaders, but no labor leaders. It heard applicants for state senator—PAC did not apply—and finally settled on Irvine Levy, Hodes' right-hand man, as its choice for party regular for state senator. With Levy in mind, Hodes met with the leaders of the other two large wards in the district, Plunkett of the Fourth and Campbell of the Twentieth. Kenneth Plunkett and Willard Campbell favored Marshall Korshak, who had been a faithful precinct worker and assistant state's attorney for years. The three ward leaders finally agreed that Levy should run for clerk of the probate court and Korshak for state senator. The county chairman gave his blessing, and a party "regular" was born.

Why was Korshak acceptable to the party? First, he could win. During his twenty years of party work, he had built a network of connections and obligations with local politicians, interest groups, and newspapers. He had the contacts, financial resources, and experience necessary to run a campaign without being a drain on the party. Second, he had earned the reputation of a "loyal" Democrat. His selection was more than a reward for past efforts. It was recognition of the fact that he understood, accepted, and would continue to build the machine. A PAC candidate could give no such promise. Furthermore, in order to keep his precinct workers busy and satisfied, a ward leader must provide them with some opportunities for office. As Hodes, Fifth Ward leader, commented, "I have no particular preference about candidates, but I do want to protect the organization. Independents can't expect to pop up at campaign time and be considered" (interview, February 12, 1951). Finally, Korshak kept his "ear to the ground" for issues which would interest his constituents. He had no personal record on legislative issues, but he had been active on civil rights as state's attorney and as a member of the Anti-Defamation League. He was therefore acceptable in the interracial and relatively liberal climate of the Fifth Senatorial District.

About six months before the primary, the Independent Voters of Illinois (IVI), Chicago affiliate of the Americans for Democratic Action, selected Alexander Elson as their "favorite son." The state PAC settled on its legal counsel, Abraham Brussel. The First Congressional District PAC however, took up the cause of Willoughby Abner, its own leader. Abner, an intelligent, ambitious, young Negro lawyer, was president of an Automobile Workers local and founder of the First District PAC. Each of these groups thought the party should make its favorite son the party regular in return for its Democratic support in 1948. But Democratic ward leaders turned a deaf ear. Republican ward leaders also found these candidates "impossible." Both machines preferred more "loyal" candidates.

Brussel and Elson refused to make the primary run without party backing. But Abner was not so bashful. The IVI was willing to indorse Abner, since its precinct workers cost nothing and it could still back Korshak against the Republican in the general election. But the state PAC was doubtful. It would have to foot Abner's bills, and it wondered whether PAC should expose its strength by a showdown at this point. The state PAC made one more plea to the Democratic party to accept its candidate. It asked the county Democratic chairman, Arvey himself, to reverse the ward leaders' decision on Korshak and to back Abner. Arvey refused. When PAC heard of IVI's indorsement, it decided to take the risk. Abner filed in the Democratic primaries against Korshak.

PAC's action was its protest to the fact that it got so little recognition on inner party councils. If it won the primary, the party would have to take its candidate. Even if it lost, PAC felt that its competition might force Korshak to commit himself more outspokenly on labor issues.

Other internal party decisions.—PAC might try to influence the selection of a party candidate by fighting at the primaries. But other internal party decisions were not laid open to external interest groups at the polls. PAC could exert little pressure on ward leaders when it came to appointing precinct captains, building party organization, disciplining factions, or distributing patronage.

Abner versus Korshak

This campaign differs from the others studied. In Chicago, PAC was not co-operating with the party to fight a Republican; it was using everything it had to defeat a Democrat. How did PAC's campaign compare with that of the party?

Rasing campaign funds.—A serious campaign is an expensive proposition in the Fifth Senatorial District. More was spent on the primary campaign in these five wards of Chicago than was spent for the entire congressional campaign in all of Jefferson County. The Independent Citizens Committee (largely IVI) contributed $3,316.21, the state PAC $5,000.00 and international and local unions $4,000.00—making a total of $12,316.21. In addition, Abner received the voluntary services of IVI precinct captains, University of Chicago students, and union staff personnel.

Customarily, regular party candidates pay for their own campaigns with contributions from their friends. Korshak's friends raised about $15,000.00. Like other Democratic candidates, Korshak had the support of party precinct organization and workers.

But the party evidently felt that several of its regular candidates faced unusually severe competition in the Fifth District in 1950. IVI and PAC sources claim that the county party chairman gave Fifth District ward leaders about $20,000.00 shortly before primary election day. If this is true, Korshak had almost three times as much to spend as Abner. PAC's competition forced the unusually heavy party contribution. In the future the party may be willing to grant PAC some voice in selecting its regular party candidate, in order to save this expense. But PAC's contribution to Abner was equally burdensome, in view of its more limited resources. PAC in the future may be more hesitant to fight the party machine over a state legislator.

Registration.—In 1948 the First Congressional District PAC staged a drive to register CIO members, but it did not repeat this in 1950. Party precinct workers went through their regular registration routine, however. One Fifth Ward precinct worker described his activities as follows:

"Registration is very important. My precinct is mobile because there are so many students and roomers in it. But I know whenever a new person moves into the neighborhood. I got sixty new registrations before this primary and eighty before the general election.

"Of course, I don't want to register Republicans. I get a line on a person's sentiments by asking around and by talking with him. If he is a Republican, I tell him he can register at the polls on election day"* [interview, February 10, 1951].

Publicity and precinct work.—Korshak had the traditional array of campaign devices: leaflets, posters, cards, buttons, matches, newspaper advertisments, speeches, banquets. PAC and IVI had the same, plus parlor meetings and weekly social gatherings in the PAC hall and bar. But all three groups relied mainly on their precinct organizations for the real work of contacting and convincing voters.

Korshak says he attended about one hundred and fifty meetings to activate and instruct small groups of precinct workers. He could count on the fact that many of these workers had already had years of political experience, that their ward leaders kept them in trim at Saturday morning pep sessions, and that their tangible rewards would inspire them to some effort.

Party precinct workers varied their campaign techniques to fit their neighborhoods, but a description of this particular campaign by one successful Democratic precinct captain must suffice:

"I am a lawyer and prosecuting attorney for the city. I have spent nineteen years in precinct work and have lived and worked in my present precinct for three and a half years.

"I try to establish a relationship of personal obligation with my people, mostly small shopkeepers and 80 per cent Jewish. I spend two or three evenings a week all year round visiting people, playing cards, talking, and helping them with their problems. My wife doesn't like this, but it is in my blood now. I know 90 per cent of my people by their first names.

* An impossibility, in fact.

"Actually, I consider myself a social service worker for my precinct. I help my people get relief and driveway permits. I help them out of unfair parking fines and property assessments. The last is most effective in my neighborhood.

"The only return I ask is that they register and vote. If they have their own opinions on certain top offices, I just ask them to vote my way on lower offices, where they usually have no preferences anyway.

"I never take leaflets or mention issues or conduct rallies in my precinct. This is a question of personal friendship between me and my neighbors. I had 260 promises for Korshak in this primary.

"On election day I paid forty or fifty people to help me because this was a 'hot' campaign. All they had to do was to get out their family and friends. I used to lease an apartment near the poll where I gave out cigars and drinks, but I don't do this any more.

"I stayed inside the poll most of election day, especially during the vote counting. If something went wrong, you could have heard me yell all over the precinct. Actually, there isn't as much fraud now as there used to be.

"Abner was not really a threat in my precinct. He had seven workers, but they contacted only their friends. No one feels obligated to them, and they worked only during the campaign. Abner's campaigners were naïve. They expected to influence people by issues, and they depended on leaflets and newspaper publicity, which isn't effective. Besides, Abner [Negro] is not hard to beat in a white precinct. I just carried a picture of both candidates around with me.

"I can control my primary vote for sure because I can make the regulars come out. I don't encourage a high vote, just a sure vote. In the general election there is much more independent voting, and I can't be sure of control" (interview, February 10, 1951).

The party had precinct workers in all Fifth Senatorial District precincts. PAC and IVI together covered 322 precincts. But Abner's workers differed from party workers both in experience and in technique. IVI had voluntary precinct workers in part of the Fourth Ward and most of the Fifth Ward. Some of them had been active in their precincts for several years, while others were new. They generally visited their neighbors only at campaign time and talked about issues rather than personal friendship. Abner won in 28 of the precincts manned by IVI.

Some of PAC's precinct workers had had campaign experience in 1948. A few had attended a community counseling course in 1950 to learn to give social agency referrals. But the majority of PAC's 212 precinct workers were completely new to this form of political action. They were given six weekly political-action meetings, a list of CIO members in their precincts, an instruction sheet, free advice, and ten dollars on election day. In return they were asked to contact the 450 voters in their precincts, beginning with CIO members. That was expecting a lot. Ten dollars was not a great incentive. PAC workers did not have so thorough a grasp of political issues as did IVI workers, and voters in PAC areas were not so independent in their voting habits as were those in IVI areas. Abner won in 38 of the 212 precincts manned by PAC.

Party workers characterized their opponents as "inexperienced," "naïve," and "undisciplined." They insisted that no one would shoulder the discipline and routine of year-round precinct work simply from an interest in issues. These comments had some validity. The 1950 precinct work of IVI and PAC did not match that of the party in intensity or coverage. Nevertheless, PAC and IVI could boast of 9,500 primary votes in direct opposition to the party. They felt that their competition strengthened Korshak's liberal legislative commitments. And they have been able not only to maintain, but even to expand, their precinct organizations without patronage for the last few years.

Contacting interest groups.—From his years as assistant state's attorney and with the backing of the firmly established machine, Korshak had good individual and group contacts in the district. He had the support of William Dawson, First District congressman and leading figure in Negro politics. The AF of L's Association of Negro Trade Unionists indorsed Korshak. Businessmen's organizations on Fifty-third, Fifty-fifth, and Sixty-third streets decided that Korshak was their man, and the Negro Chamber of Commerce, to which 75 per cent of Negro businesses belong, gave him informal support. No direct connection could be established between Korshak and the syndicates, but these groups have been known to make generous contributions to hard-pressed party precinct captains. Korshak even got a sympathetic hearing from the prominent Negro newspaper, the *Defender*.

Abner was an upstart by comparison. Leaders of the Illinois Association for the Advancement of Colored People and the Urban League helped him as individuals, but their organizations made no formal indorsements. Business groups bypassed him completely. Abner spoke to the Negro Ministerial Alliance, but this group made no commitments. He did, however, get the backing of the *Daily News* and the *Sun-Times*. The University of Chicago was Abner territory. Students formed a Campus Committee for Abner, which helped staff his office, and faculty members were prominent on the Citizens Committee for Abner, which helped raise funds.

Abner's most important ally was IVI, which, like PAC, had

built its own independent precinct organization. Without both PAC and IVI precinct organizations, a serious campaign would have been unthinkable. PAC and IVI divided their precinct responsibility at Cottage Grove Avenue but co-ordinated their strategy at weekly meetings. PAC's research director and Abner himself were members of IVI's executive board. Altogether, IVI precincts were responsible for about half of Abner's vote.

Election-day work.—A party regular, like Korshak, had several advantages on election day. His name appeared on the top lever of the voting machine for Democratic voters. According to law, one representative from each party could enter the booth with a voter upon request, and the Democrat was naturally a regular. Polling officials were designated by the regular parties. The city election board itself was composed of regular Republicans and Democrats. Independents felt that the board was not duly responsive to their queries and pleas for help during election day.

Korshak's real advantage, however, was his experienced poll watchers, many of whom were well versed in election law, the challenging rights of the parties, and the numerous possibilities for error and fraud. Abner had hoped to have three election-day workers of his own in each precinct. Actually, he had about three hundred, spread unevenly through the 361 precincts. It was the first election-day experience for most of them. They were shown a United Automobile Workers' film on vote-counting, but unfortunaely no film can introduce a person to the possibilities of Chicago elections. PAC workers were not sure of their rights when unauthorized persons entered the polls, when voting machines jammed, or when judges asked voters to leave their preferences on slips of paper to be entered later in the machines. PAC probably did lose some legitimate votes on election day, though not enough to change the outcome of the election. PAC workers will have to have considerably more experience before they become effective "watchdogs" at the polls.

For a young organization, PAC put up a good primary fight. But it could not match the party in funds, precinct work, connections, or poll watchers. Despite its best efforts, Abner was defeated 21,739 to 9,537.

Advantages and Limitations of a Primary Fight

Running a PAC candidate against a party regular had one obvious advantage from PAC's point of view. If its candidate succeeded, PAC would not be caught with the "lesser of two evils." In the Fifth Senatorial District, moreover, a Democratic candidate, once nominated, had more than an even chance of final election. He was over the highest hurdle toward PAC's real goal—the election of a public official committed to PAC issues.

Second, even though it might not win, a primary run gave PAC a chance to exhibit its independent strength. The party and candidate might be sufficiently impressed by the liberal vote to remember the issues they represented. Rather than risk another expensive battle, the party might let PAC help select the party regular. While Abner's 9,500 votes could not nearly win a primary, they could almost have swung the final election. Someday a party might be willing to bargain for a bloc.

And, finally, an independent campaign, successful or not, had concrete educational value. PAC leaders and precinct workers needed to develop experience at the polls and contacts in the neighborhoods. Rank-and-file workers needed to learn about independent voting behavior. In an independent primary campaign PAC could not depend on Democratic workers to carry the load.

But a primary relationship also presented serious limitations. First, it cost a lot and did not attain its real objective—Abner's primary election. A heavy investment in an independent candidate in the Fifth Senatorial District was a risky venture, to say the least. PAC's limited money and leadership might have been used to better advantage in communities where a PAC candidate had a better chance of actual election or where the party regular was more "reactionary" than Korshak.

Second, it is debatable whether PAC, in this case, exposed its strength or its weakness. Two party ward leaders claimed they had assumed that PAC was worth more than the 9,500 votes it actually got. A primary showdown was advantageous to PAC only if party leaders had underestimated its strength. If they had overestimated, PAC might have done better to keep its actual strength a mystery.

Third, PAC ran the risk of inducing a hostile, rather than a co-operative, mood in the party. The machine might decide that PAC's demands were a threat to its own and that it would be wiser to weaken, rather than consort with, this "unreliable" group. A hostile party might not only refuse to grant PAC concessions but deliberately weaken it by anti-PAC rumors in the precincts, by gerrymandering, or by influence in the legislature. After Abner's campaign, however, party leaders seemed to be less concerned, rather than more worried, about the political strength of organized labor.

Finally, the concessions that a machine can make to any independent group, no matter how strong, are limited. The Chicago machine is controlled by a patronage interest group. This group could afford to adopt legislative issues which did not seriously affect its own objectives or position of control. But PAC could not expect the party to accept candidates hostile to the machine, to promote electoral reforms which might jeopardize its position of control, or to share its control over basic party decisions. No machine wants to commit suicide. Such basic changes could be brought about only by groups strong enough and responsible enough to take over the party.

Why Did PAC Fight the Party in Chicago?

PAC might have tried supplementing Korshak, electing ward leaders, balancing power, or running Abner at the general election. Why did it choose to fight the party at the primary, instead?

The election district.—PAC had a permanent organization and concentrated membership only in that half of the Fifth Senatorial District which lay in the First Congressional District. IVI had its organization and membership largely in that half of the Fifth District which lay in the Second Congressional District. Any liberal political action in the Fifth District thus required the support of both groups. IVI showed little inclination toward third-party or internal party activity, but it was willing to support Abner as an independent in the primaries. This was the only party relationship, therefore, upon which the necessary liberals could agree.

Election practices.—The practice of appointing, rather than electing, precinct captains made it very difficult for PAC to enter the party with any control. If precinct captains had been selected at the primaries, PAC might have been able to elect fifty-six, in those precincts where Abner showed a lead over Korshak. It might even have formed an internal party coalition capable of controlling the ward party. But, since only ward leaders were up for election, PAC would have had to produce a majority in the entire ward to get any internal party representation at all. PAC was not prepared for such an expensive undertaking.

A second election practice which made influence difficult for PAC was the designation of party regulars. While the primary theoretically opened the nomination of party candidates to any voter, the system of regulars put candidates of party groups at a considerable advantage. Far more resources were required to win a primary in Chicago than in communities in which there was free competition for party nomination.

Voting behavior.—Unfortunately, relevant statistics for the Fifth Senatorial District are available only since 1947, when there was complete redistricting. General election votes for state representative and senators in 1948 and 1950 indicate that PAC might have been able to shift the outcome of the election by swinging about 10,000 votes. A balance of power thus seemed within the range of possibility for PAC and IVI, which together could raise 9,500 votes in the primary. Evidently, they did not rely on this method of action, because they found neither the Republican nor the Democratic candidate acceptable and because they estimated that they had the votes to elect a primary candidate of their own.

Did it seem realistic for PAC to run its independent against this regular in the Democratic primary? Primary votes for state representative and senator in 1948 and 1950 would indicate that between 22,000 and 36,000 votes would be necessary to elect an independent against a party regular. This required vote seems high in terms of PAC's 10,000 district membership and its lack of support from the AF of L.

PAC might, of course, have entered its candidate in the Republican primary for state senator. It could have won this contest with only 10,573 votes in 1950. But it may have doubted its ability to get its liberal followers out to a Republican primary. Also it knew that a Democrat had a better chance of final election than a Republican; the Fifth District has returned Democratic state senators since 1936, with only one exception.

If PAC had run Abner at the general election rather than at the primary, it would have fallen into the category of a third party. Third parties have never made a good showing in this part of Chicago. The 1948 Wallace Progressive candidate for Congress got only 5,669 votes in the First Congressional District, compared to Democrat William Dawson's 98,690. Maynard Krueger, who ran as an independent in the Second Congressional District in 1948, got 4,566 votes as compared to Democrat Barratt O'Hara's 91,648. A serious third-party candidate for state senator in 1950 would have needed at least 50,000 votes, a very unlikely possibility for PAC and IVI.

Since the county party chairman can effectively designate or remove a ward leader by directing patronage, interest groups have seldom tried this road to party power. In 1948, when ward leaders were up for election, there were no contests for the office in the three largest wards of the Fifth Senatorial District. A comparison of Abner's vote in 1950 with votes for ward leaders in 1948 indicates that PAC and IVI could not turn out enough votes to elect a ward leader in any case. A successful effort would require over 6,000 votes per ward, whereas Abner got no more than 3,000.

Compatible interest groups.—Since PAC had only a rudimentary organization in half of the Fifth District, it had to depend on support from friendly interest groups for a successful primary campaign. Were its hopes realistic?

The Fifth District has unusually sharp ethnic divisions, being about 60 per cent Negro and 15 per cent Jewish. As a Negro himself, Abner may have expected some support from his ethnic group. Unlike Ohio, however, the Negro community in

Chicago was already fairly well organized politically by the Democratic machine. While the party may have exploited racial tensions at the precinct level (see p. 68), it was wise enough to avoid such factions at ward and district levels. Abner got less than half his vote from Negro wards. Abner had contact with liberal Jewish leaders, but Korshak had the advantage of membership in this congregation.

One Negro YMCA leader commented, "We are a working-class community." Korshak estimated that 50,000 of the 65,000 employed in Negro areas belonged to unions, especially steel, packing, auto, transport, building, and hotel and restaurant workers. Unfortunately for Abner, however, this potential was poorly aroused politically and anything but united. That part of the AF of L which was politically conscious backed the machine. The CIO had about 10,000 members, but not all these favored Abner.

Other interest groups, known for other political influence, were the gambling establishments. Bookmakers existed with apparent impunity in some of the large hotels along the lake in the white community. In the Negro neighborhoods policy was a favorite gambling medium. As in Steubenville, the syndicates offered financial resources to either party in return for protection, especially from sheriff and police officers. They did not make big payoffs to the parties or run gamblers for public office. Local establishments simply gave generously to hard-pressed precinct workers who found that money was very hard to get from business, labor, or ethnic groups. The syndicates were also ready to subsidize needy candidates. However, gambling was not greatly condemned in public opinion. "Mush-mouth" Johnson, Robert T. Motts, and Dan Jackson, former gambling kings, were, as often as not, admired for their ability to "beat the economic system." The machine, already in a position of power, was obviously better able to tap this source of funds than PAC, with little political influence, and IVI, with its reform objectives.

Protestant churches conducted considerably more political activity in the Negro than in the white community. But Korshak spoke from five times as many pulpits as Abner did. In general, the churches did not act as an effective resource for independent liberals.

Fortunately for Abner, however, the Fifth District was rich in independent voters, especially in the Fourth and Fifth wards around the University of Chicago. They had their own active interest group—IVI. A quarter of IVI's total Chicago membership was located in the Fifth Ward. The Fifth Senatorial District thus contained social groupings with potentially liberal interests, but these groups were not lying fallow. The Democratic party already had deep tap roots among them, and PAC found these hard to cut. As a result, PAC had difficulty finding sufficient political support for independent primary activity, and third-party activity was out of the question.

Composition and objectives of the machine.—In 1948, 80 per cent of Chicago's ward leaders derived ther incomes from government jobs, and 70 per cent of Chicago's precinct captains were on public pay rolls. "Patronage," commented Gosnell in his book *Machine Politics*, "is the cement which unites the party organization." The Cook County party has been known to suffer internal strife over the division of spoils, but in 1950 one patronage group under Arvey, the county party chairman, seemed to have factions well in hand. What was the relationship of groups with other interests to this patronage machine? The machine needed the support of other interest groups to win a general election. To capture their vote and financial support, it was willing to grant concessions: sometimes protection, sometimes a reform candidate, sometimes a liberal issue. But one thing it could not afford to jeopardize—its own position of control.

Party leaders were not personally hostile to PAC; neither were they personally in sympathy with it. They treated it as they treated any interest group, dealing with it if its political resources were important and rejecting it if it demanded too much. In the Fifth District the party could well afford to run a liberal candidate. But, when PAC and IVI demanded an effective voice in nominations and pushed their own antimachine or reform candidates, the machine felt threatened. Such demands jeopardized the position of its dominant interest group. PAC and the party then found themselves at sword's point.

PAC objectives.—What were the objectives of the First Congressional District PAC? Did they make PAC incompatible with the patronage-minded rulers of the party machine?

Like other PAC's, the First District PAC accepted the immediate legislative goals laid down at state and national CIO conventions. PAC was admittedly designed to help elect candidates favorable to these issues. Why then, did it challenge Korshak, who was willing to vote liberal in the state legislature?

Whether it admitted so officially or not, the First District PAC was interested in more than a liberal candidate. One of its unofficial objectives came to light at the Illinois state PAC convention. On February 18, 1950, the *Daily News* reported:

"The CIO Political Action Committee has served notice on the Democrats that it wants a bigger voice in Party affairs. This marks the first public sign of revolt by the labor group against the Democrats. While the PAC has supported some Republicans, most of its activity has been for the benefit of Democratic candidates. . . . Meeting in a two day conference at the Morrison Hotel the state group complained that it had received 'no patronage and no voice in slatemaking in several counties,' despite election work."

In other words, PAC wanted a share of party control and a voice in selecting party regulars. This was too much for Fifth Ward Chairman Hodes, Fourth Ward Chairman Plunkett, and County Chairman Arvey. While they could accept liberals like Korshak, they could not risk backing a PAC candidate like Abner, whose basic loyalty was to PAC rather than to the party machine and who might even use his legislative influence to weaken the machine. With this demand, PAC and the party became incompatible.

Second, the Independent Voters of Illinois and, to a lesser extent, PAC were skeptical of the connection of the party and the candidate with the syndicates. IVI adopted "clean government" as one of its objectives. PAC did not officially admit to reform motives, but its leaders and members did seem to feel embarrassed when caught holding hands with protection groups inside the party. The state PAC research director wrote in a report dated December 28, 1950:

"I have been opposed generally to trying to fight both the battle for clean government and the battle for a liberal program at the same time, on the theory that we disperse our energies too much and that the two issues are not exactly the same, nor are they supported by exactly the same people. But the Gilbert business here in Chicago makes me think that even if we don't engage actively in a clean government campaign, we would do well not to ignore the issue it can be."* The Steubenville PAC had not adopted a reform objective and could thus establish a friendly balance of power with the party. But when Abner's precinct workers started worrying about Kor-

*The "Gilbert business" refers to the fact that PAC indorsed Gilbert, a Democrat, for sheriff in the 1950 election. The newspapers called him "the richest policeman in the world" and claimed his prosperity was derived from the syndicates. He was defeated.

shak's connections, they admitted their incompatibility not only
with him but with the party.

And, finally, the PAC leader could not help thinking about
third parties. Abner hoped his independent ward and precinct
organization might someday form the basis for such a party.
Such ideas naturally looked dangerous to Democratic machine
leaders. It was not surprising that they refused to put Abner
on their slate as a regular. In their eyes he was patently disloyal. A PAC with a third party in the back of its mind must
expect to meet the party head-on, sooner or later.

The objectives of PAC and the Democratic machine in the
Fifth Senatorial District were too different to avoid collision.

The structure of PAC.—Did the First District PAC have a
structure in 1950 capable of taking on the party? This district
PAC was probably the most active in Illinois. But its organization covered only half of the Fifth Senatorial District and
was inexperienced even there. Abner hoped in the future to
establish neighborhood clubs in PAC areas. These clubs would
not only raise money to keep the district PAC organization
alive but would also service the precincts. Abner envisioned
them as social and recreational centers for voters from any
party. In the course of club activities, voters would be exposed
to liberal and independent political ideas. Furthermore, Abner
hoped to have a regular CIO community service worker at each
club to refer needy voters to the proper social agencies for
help. If such a program did develop extensively, PAC might
have a service organization in the precincts able to challenge
that of the party. But such clubs were not yet in existence
in 1950. PAC overestimated its capacity even for a primary
battle.

The business of the district PAC, according to its by-laws,
was conducted by a steering committee, "consisting of the
officers, all area leaders, and representatives designated by those

local unions with membership in the district, . . . together with the chairmen of all committees." This steering committee met weekly throughout 1950, though attendance was not always high. State PAC by-laws stipulated that the Congressional District PAC should have no policy-making power. Only the state PAC had final power to indorse candidates for state offices and to formulate methods of political action. The PAC of the Cook County Industrial Union Council had power to make local indorsements and to co-ordinate the congressional district PAC's within its jurisdiction. The steering committee of the district PAC was merely an executive arm to build precinct organization and organize voters.

First District PAC workers were not completely happy about this distribution of authority. As the people who pushed the doorbells, they felt they knew their district better han county and state council representatives, few of whom even lived in the district. They therefore wanted a voice in indorsements and political-action policy. County and state PAC's generally accepted district PAC suggestions. But in Abner's case the state was not enthusiastic about a primary campaign.

Composition of PAC.—What were PAC's human resources? Did it have the experienced leaders, hard workers, and interested voters necessary for the more influential forms of political activity?

Abner, the district PAC leader, was an able and energetic young man, bitterly anti-Communist in outlook but imbued with a militant labor-conscious idealism rather than the pragmatism of Steubenville. He had a vision of labor with a share of political control rather than a few crumbs dropped from the party's table. The idea of a labor party appealed to him. He himself was a product of the hard economic life of the First Congressional District. He went to law school while working in a local automobile plant. He had fairly close personal contact with local people, customs, and problems. His political experience was largely in the melee of UAW politics, at which he had proved quite succesful. He connected himself quickly with all levels of the PAC hierarchy as leader of the First Congressional District PAC, vice-president of the Cook County Industrial Union Council, regional political-action director of UAW, and representative to the state PAC. He was a hard-driving, ambitious, intellectual type of leader, without an easy-going personal touch. He built and managed the district PAC organization and his own campaign practically single-handed. Under his energetic leadership it is not surprising that the district PAC attempted to challenge the Democratic party in 1950.

PAC ward, area, and precinct workers caught Abner's enthusiasm for independent political action, but they did not arise in great numbers. They were intensely loyal to Abner, but they had little political experience. They needed more confidence and know-how before they could hope to face party workers with an even chance.

The average voter in the Fifth Senatorial District did not suffer from Ohio's great suspicion of labor in politics. Especially in the Negro community, labor organizations were considered quite respectable. But the average voter was thoroughly impressed with the strength of the Democratic machine. He may have been on the receiving end of some of its attentions himself. Challenging the machine seemed a little like questioning God. As in other cases, PAC had to bestir itself to get CIO members out to vote.

One of the greatest drains on district PAC's political resources, however, was internal factionalism. CIO unions had different ideas about political action and were in different stages of development. When the state PAC asked for membership lists from its constituent CIO unions, steel, auto, textile, and some packinghouse locals complied. Clothing, electrical, and shipbuilding locals did not. As a result, the district PAC was not even sure of support from its own membership. An even graver problem arose from the fact that not all CIO unions wanted Abner as district leader or approved of his independent political action. Many large packinghouse locals were still considered "left-wing" and refused to co-operate with Abner's bitter anti-communism. The United Transport Service Employees, whose international headquarters was in the First Congressional District, disagreed with Abner's antimachine approach. Williard Townsend, its president and also a vice-president of the national CIO, favored closer co-operation with the Democratic party and considered Abner's more radical demands and independent activity foolhardy. He and Abner may also have felt themselves in personal competition for influence in the Negro community. As a result of this conflict, Abner refused to locate PAC headquarters in the Transport Services building, and Townsend made no reference to Abner in his weekly articles in the *Defender* at campaign time. Such internal differences weakened PAC at a time when every dollar and every vote were needed to beat the better-disciplined machine.

Summary

In the Fifth Senatorial District of Illinois, PAC did not enter the Democratic party. Instead, it built an independent political organization among CIO members, which it could direct at the party's soft spots. But, unfortunately for PAC, the party was not soft. PAC's independent organization had little influence on internal party decisions, such as the choice of party regulars and the distribution of patronage. PAC decided to challenge the machine on the state senatorial nomination, a question that was laid open to outsiders by the primary. PAC put on a lively campaign and forced the party to spend more than usual to defend its regular. But PAC did not have the funds, the contacts, and the experienced workers that the party had been able to develop over the years. Its candidate was decisively defeated.

A primary relationship had certain advantages for PAC. If it had been able to get Abner on the Democratic slate, he would have had a good chance of final election. PAC could exhibit its voting strength to the party and train its own workers and members. A primary relationship also had limitations. The state PAC spent its money in a situation where its chances of success were not good. The showdown may have impressed the party with PAC's weakness rather than its strength. PAC ran the risk of incurring powerful enemies, and, moreover, the patronage-oriented party was limited in the concessions it could grant.

PAC adopted a primary relationship because other forms of pressure seemed unsatisfactory or impossible. If PAC had supplemented the party or balanced power, it would have had to be content with party regulars. Capturing a share of internal party control was too costly to be a realistic alternative. The party was too strong. A third party in 1950 was out of the question. PAC had only half the district organized, its workers were untrained, and its contacts with supporting interests poor. The only alternative was a primary challenge, and even this was risky. Party regulars had the advantage of election practices and a strong organization in the precincts. PAC did not have AF of L support, and CIO unions were not all equally enthusiastic about the idea. Nevertheless, the strong leadership of Abner, the loyalty of his followers, and the enthusiasm of the Independent Voters of Illinois drew PAC into the primary fight.

V Rockford: PAC Enters
a County Party

AT THE same primary in which the First District PAC was
locked in a bitter struggle with the powerful Chicago machine,
the Sixteenth Congressional District PAC, not one hundred
miles away, was experimenting with an entirely different
method of political action (see Fig. 3).

Instead of building an independent ward and precinct organization like those in Steubenville and Chicago, the Rockford
PAC decided to use its influence to make the existing Democratic organization a better vehicle for PAC objectives. Patronage groups had long made party organization a medium
for job-hunting; why shouldn't PAC use it to promote its
legislative issues?

The Sixteenth Congressional District lies in the northwestern
corner of Illinois. Six of its seven counties are rural, but the
seventh, Winnebago County, contains Illinois's third-largest
and fastest-growing industrial city, Rockford. The rural counties are staunchly Republican in outlook. The district has not
elected a Democratic congressman since the Civil War. But
Rockford, with its labor and minority groups, has a considerable Democratic vote and a large Democratic potential. This
is a study of the relationship which the Sixteenth District PAC
established with the Winnebago County Democratic party at
the time of Russell Goldman's campaign for Congress.

Jo Daviess Stephenson Winnebago
                                ○ROCKFORD

Carroll 16 Ogle

Whiteside Lee

○CHICAGO

SPRINGFIELD
⊙

SIXTEENTH
CONGRESSIONAL
DISTRICT
OF ILLINOIS

FIG. 3

PAC Enters the Winnebago County Democratic Party

The idea of influencing the party from inside occurred to an active and able United Automobile Workers (UAW) representative, Willard Allen, who had been servicing locals around Rockford for several years. Specifically, he wanted to enter candidates for captain in as many of Winnebago County's 146 precincts as possible, and to run Russell Goldman, a labor lawyer, for congressman from the Sixteenth District. He presented this plan to the state PAC on December 30, 1949. This body agreed to let him try it and appointed him district leader. Back in Rockford, he pulled together a 104-man PAC which officially undertook the project at a breakfast on January 8, 1950. This left only twelve days to find PAC precinct captains and to enter their names with the city clerk. Forty-five candidates, mostly members of PAC, were hastily indorsed.

Since few of these PAC candidates had run for precinct captain before, the PAC leader had to give them considerable help. He organized a series of eight classes on political action and provided PAC's candidates with calling cards, precinct lists, mimeographed letters, publicity in the labor paper, and advice.

The April 11 primary returned 27 PAC-indorsed precinct captains, carrying about 1,400 such Democratic votes. (In Winnebago County a precinct captain carries a vote equal to the Democratic ballots cast in his precinct in the primary.) But it also showed that other groups had been busy electing precinct captains. Since the total committee vote was about 5,700, it would take about 2,800 votes to elect a county chairman. PAC could expect about 1,925 votes from groups 1 and 3 (Table 2). Its sure opposition—groups 4 and 5—had only 550 votes. But 1,850 votes were an unknown quantity. PAC had to make a coalition if it was to be sure of electing sympathetic party officers. Edward Hunter, leader of one patronage group inside the party and party chairman since 1948, had, as state representative, voted against a state fair employment practices act. PAC

TABLE 2

INTEREST GROUPS ON THE WINNEBAGO COUNTY CENTRAL
DEMOCRATIC COMMITTEE, APRIL, 1950

Group	Primary Objective	Interest Groups Represented	Precinct Captains	Vote (Approx.)
1........	Liberal issues	PAC	27	1,400
2........	Patronage	All American Club	13	1,375
3........	Liberal issues	Independent liberals and some AF of L	14	525
4........	Patronage	Hunter faction	12	300
5........	Opposition to CIO	Expelled CIO unions, some AF of L, Knights of Columbus	9	250
6........	Unknown	....	48	1,850
Vacant precincts...	....	....	23	....
Total..	....	....	146	5,700

therefore decided to make its arrangements with the All American Club, an Italian group.

The All American Club did not have the same interests as PAC, its members being primarily concerned with the fifty-four state jobs at the disposal of a party chairman. An All American ran against PAC for state representative in the primary and lost by only 113 votes. But at least the club had not committed itself against PAC issues. The two groups could combine their political resources without conceding much on their objectives. At closed caucus meetings between April 12 and April 24 the "deal" was arranged. PAC agreed to support Guzzardo of the All American Club for party chairman in return for All American support of PAC candidates for secretary and the patronage committee. Hunter, failing to caucus significant opposition, offered to give up his bid for chairman if the PAC–All American coalition would back a "neutral" candidate. But the coalition had sufficient votes to refuse this compromise. At the County Democratic Convention on April 24 the coalition came into power by a vote of 3,256 to 2,205. Guzzardo became chairman, and the district PAC director, secretary. PAC got three places out of nine on the important patronage committee. Together, the coalition held twenty-six committee places, and the opposition only seven. The coalition had all the party officers. Rockford's only Republican newspaper announced next morning: "The election gave Rockford labor virtual control of the Democratic Party here."

PAC and Internal Party Decisions

As a result of this primary victory, PAC won a direct voice in internal party councils. It did not hesitate to raise it. PAC's influence can be estimated by comparing the Winnebago County party in 1950 with the party as it had functioned in previous years.

Selecting party candidates.—The Winnebago County Democratic party, though the most important in the Sixteenth District, has never been noted for great activity. The district has not produced a Democratic congressman since before the Civil War. In the late 1920's the Winnebago party gave up running candidates for county offices. With the Roosevelt boom, the county party came to life for a while, filling its precincts, slating candidates, and even winning a few local victories. But it declined again in the 1940's and by 1950 was again unable to find anyone willing to run for county offices on the Democratic ticket.

A few days before the 1950 primary, the PAC–All American coalition decided that the party ballot should have no blanks. They persuaded a few lawyers to act as "sacrificial goats" (candidates who have little chance of winning but run to

TABLE 3

INTEREST GROUPS REPRESENTED ON THE WINNEBAGO DEMO-
CRATIC PRIMARY BALLOT, APRIL, 1950

Office	Candidate	Interest Group	Outcome
Congressman, 16th District...	Myrland	Hunter faction	Lost
	Goldman	PAC	Won
State representative, 10th Senatorial District....... (Select 2)	Hunter	Hunter faction	Won
	Barbagello	All American Club	Lost
	Fenelon	Unknown	Lost
	Pierce	PAC	Won
	Tyler	Unknown	Lost

strengthen party organization) and prepared a slate of "stick-in" candidates (whose names are pasted in by the voters) for county offices. To meet this unexpected competition, the Hunter faction also rounded up a slate at the last moment. The coalition won four of its five county candidates in the primary.

The Winnebago party designated no regulars, as in Chicago. As a result, the primary ballot looked like a roster of its internal interest groups (see Table 3).

PAC indorsed its candidates for congressman and state representative at the meeting at which it decided to enter the party. Russell Goldman, PAC's candidate for Congress, was a liberal labor lawyer, well known in Rockford. Bill Pierce, its

selection for state representative, was president of a large
UAW local. PAC and Hunter factions thus opposed each other
over party candidates as well as over precinct captains in the
primary. PAC succeeded in electing both Goldman and Pierce
in the primary. But Hunter himself became one of the two
Democratic candidates for state representative from the Tenth
Senatorial District. PAC thus played a significant role in the
Democratic primary, nominating county officers, congressman,
and one of the two state representatives.

Strengthening party organization.—During the Roosevelt era,
when county party organization was fairly strong, there were
no Democratic precinct vacancies in Rockford. In many precincts several people contended for these jobs, thus insuring
party activity. By 1948, however, a quarter of Winnebago's
precincts lay vacant, and there were few contests for precinct
jobs. PAC's activity in 1950 considerably strengthened the
party's precinct coverage. The number of vacant precincts declined from twenty-eight to nineteen, and the number of con-
tested precincts rose from eighteen to thirty-one.

Party discipline.—Until 1948 the Winnebago County Democratic party had been composed of three fairly well-defined
patronage-oriented groups—the Old Line Democrats, who were
in control of the party; the Hunter faction, which objected to
their division of patronage; and the All American Democratic
Club, an active Italian group. In the years from 1944 to 1948
these factions bickered continually among themselves. The
Hunter faction and the All American Club, irate over patronage, finally formed a Good Fellowship coalition, which split
the party.

In 1948 the party chairman, an Old Line Democrat, resigned
to take a state job. Thereupon, the Good Fellowship coalition
broke apart. Guzzardo of the All American Club fought

Hunter for the party chairmanship. Hunter won, but at the price of the undying hostility of the All Americans. At the same time, he was elected state representative. This gave him little time for county party responsibilities. When he violated the state party line by voting against a fair employment practices bill in the state legislature, he incurred the hostility of the State Democratic Committee and received less patronage to distribute. As a result, the party was weak and factionalized when PAC entered in 1950.

The advent of PAC into the party helped resolve these particular factional difficulties. The All American Club found that it could work in coalition with PAC. Together they discovered that they could get rid of the Hunter faction. The coalition vote was sufficient to depose Hunter as party chairman. By virtue of its control over the patronage committee, the coalition removed Hunter's men from state jobs. And the coalition campaigned against Hunter for state representative at the general election with as much enthusiasm as it fought Republicans. Because of their success in the primary, both Hunter and Pierce were up for state representative on the Democratic ticket at the general election. According to Illinois electoral law, a Democratic voter had the option of casting either three votes for Hunter or for Pierce, or else one and one-half votes for each. The coalition conducted a campaign for "three votes for Pierce," which rivaled its campaign against the Republicans. Hunter was defeated and did not return to the state legislature.

PAC's activity as an internal interest group thus resulted in unifying a previously weak and factionalized party.

Distributing party rewards.—The Winnebago County Democratic party has been weak because it has been run by patronage groups which had little patronage to distribute. Federal jobs did not come through the county party at all but through

Democratic Senator Lucas' law partner, who lived in Rockford. The number of state jobs available declined under Governor Stevenson, and Republicans regularly elected the county officials. The county Democratic party, therefore, had only about fifty-four state jobs at its disposal.

Final decisions regarding the distribution of this patronage, since the rise of the coalition, has rested between Guzzardo of the All American Club and Allen of PAC. Allen has not been at all enthusiastic about getting jobs for his PAC workers. Not only would this take active members out of the CIO, but it would make them subject to the fortunes of the party. He felt that they would not be willing to walk out of the party when dissatisfied. Nor have PAC members asked for patronage jobs, since they received better pay and more security in the factories.

But Allen was perfectly willing to use patronage to strengthen PAC and to weaken the opposition. Between April and November, 1950, three Democratic payrollers (patronage appointees) lost their jobs. All three were men who had run against PAC precinct captains in the primary. All vacant patronage positions were filled by All American appointees, with PAC's sanction. The party chairman himself became liquor inspector. The club was thus obligated to PAC. Allen used patronage not as an end but as a means for strengthening PAC's position.

From its coalition stronghold, PAC was thus able to exert its influence directly on selecting candidates, electing party officers, building party organization, disciplining factions, and distributing patronage.

PAC in Goldman's Campaign

With PAC prodding, the Winnebago County party put on the most vigorous off-year campaign that Rockford had seen

for some time. The Democratic congressional vote in Winnebago County rose from 14,774 in November, 1946, to 20,528
in November, 1950. What part did PAC play in the 1950 Democratic campaign?

Raising campaign funds.—In 1948 the Winnebago party is
said to have spent only $1,700 on all its campaign work. Big
Democratic donors gave tokens of their regard directly to the
state party committee. In 1950 the Democratic party, under
the direction of the coalition, sponsored a picnic, at which it
raised $3,700, all of which went to support its county slate.

PAC spent about $8,640 on its two favorite sons. Two thou-
sand dollars of this came from a successful "corn boil" sponsored by the Rockford CIO Industrial Union Council. Four
thousand dollars were contributed by CIO locals in the form
of publicity for Pierce, and reimbursement for those who took
time off from their jobs for political work. Fifteen hundred
dollars were donated by the state PAC, and $500 came from
the voluntary dollar drive. The remainder was the result of
the sale of campaign buttons and donations from the Rockford
Industrial Union Council, the State Democratic Committee,
the Ogle County AF of L, and a Jewish group in Chicago.
About three-quarters of Democratic campaign funds were thus
contributed by PAC. PAC spent its funds directly on its candidates rather than through the county Democratic committee,
and it helped its candidates in kind rather than in cash.

Registration.—In 1950 PAC was the only Democratic interest
group to make a registration drive. It checked CIO membership lists with official registration files, to locate unregistered
unionists. It gave free chances on a television set to union
members who were registered. It distributed leaflets at plant
gates, saying: "Being unregistered is like going to work without
your pants on." The UAW subregional paper, the *Advocator*,
put forth its best efforts. Since its request for mobile registra-

tion in the factories was denied, PAC rounded up cars to take unregistered members to the election board at lunch time and after union meetings. The sidewalks blossomed with signs reading, "Register To Vote on November Seventh." On precinct registration day in the sixteen suburban areas, PAC had thirty-nine people soliciting registrations from door to door.

PAC claimed that it had registered 7,200 voters in the week beginning October 10. The Rockford Board of Education reported a final net gain of 1,750, after the moved and deceased had been dropped.

Campaign publicity.—The Rockford PAC called itself the "Goldman for Congress Committee" and carried his praises to the entire Sixteenth District. Even before the primary, PAC estimates that it handed out over 100,000 pieces of literature. This included *Hometown News*, a four-page tabloid featuring Goldman, picture postcards, car stickers, calling cards, a letter from Goldman to precinct workers and payrollers, placards for telephone poles and store windows, sample ballots, "Vote Today" placards, advertisements in twenty-three newspapers, Goldman buttons, and T-shirts. None of this came from the state PAC office, as was done in Ohio.

PAC also produced some special features. On April 1 a loud-speaking motorcade toured Winnebago and Ogle counties. PAC's full-length film, *The Roosevelt Story*, showed the blessings of the welfare state to twenty-five CIO, AF of L, Grange, and party groups throughout the district. Goldman made daily trips to small towns throughout the area for several months and challenged his Republican opponent to a public debate. PAC subsidized over one hundred radio spot announcements and several longer speeches.

PAC publicity differed from previous party efforts not only in quantity but in content. It emphasized farm supports, extended social security, increased minimum wages, health insurance, public housing and civil rights—issues which had been considered "too hot to handle" by its patronage predecessors. Emphasis on such issues, however, tended to limit its support to labor, lower-income, liberal, and minority groupings.

The county party as a whole took care of publicity for the rest of the Democratic slate. It issued a twelve-page tabloid, the *Winnebago County Democrat*, arranged rallies and dinners for Douglas and Lucas, and activated its patronage holders. The climax of the Democratic campaign, however, was a colorful parade with bands, floats, and balloons for vice-president Barkley on November 2 in Rockford. Even these party activities had a PAC tinge.

Contacting interest groups.—Before 1950, the Winnebago party had never made a serious attempt to organize and arouse Swedish, Slavic, Negro, labor, and small-business interest groups.

The 1950 coalition had the initial advantage of direct contact with Italian and CIO voters. PAC tried a political-action federation with AF of L locals, but the project collapsed after three meetings. Some appeal was made to Negroes by a rally at their Legion post. A small businessman's organization indorsed Goldman. A Catholic interest group, the Knights of Columbus, was pro-Democratic but anti-PAC.

Fortunately, the Rockford PAC did not have to contend with so much community suspicion as did the Ohio PAC. Both of Rockford's daily papers were owned by a member of the McCormick family. They displayed little sympathy toward organized labor, but they did not directly "red-bait" the local CIO or PAC.

Despite these advantages, neither PAC nor the All American Club advanced far over their predecessors in co-ordinating compatible political interest groups. As a result, while the coalition had sufficient votes to capture the county party at the primary, it had by no means sufficient strength to defeat a Republican congressman at the general election.

Election-day work.—On primary election day PAC hired no workers. The Democratic party had the services of its fifty-four payrollers. PAC estimates that, of the total 4,961 Democratic primary voters, 1,700 were CIO members. In the Sixteenth Congressional District, Goldman defeated his Democratic rival, Myrland, by 990 votes, and Hunter and Pierce became Democratic candidates for the state assembly from the Tenth Senatorial District.

On November 7 the Democratic party again had the services of its payrollers. PAC hired 167 workers in addition, primarily to bring out the labor vote. Pierce was elected state representative, running 2,108½ votes ahead of Hunter. But Goldman came in 42,246 votes behind the Republican opponent, Leo Allen, in the Sixteenth Congressional District.

Under the coalition, the Winnebago County Democratic party has produced more active campaigns than previously. PAC was the spirit that moved the campaign in Rockford as much as in Ohio. But in Rockford the spirit moved under a Democratic "cover."

Advantages and Limitations of an Internal Party Relationship

PAC derived certain concrete advantages from its position inside the party. First, instead of merely supplementing a disorganized and hostile party, as in Ohio, PAC was able to make some party reforms. It shook the party into life, strengthened its precinct organization, and tossed out its hostile factions. Instead of creating another independent organization, PAC made the party itself a vehicle for labor's interests.

Second, PAC had a cover. In a rural Republican area like the Sixteenth Congressional District, a Democratic label was bad enough, but a PAC label was impossible. From its internal position, PAC could call its man Goldman a Democrat. It could get local lawyers to run on the Democratic ballot who would not think of associating themselves with a third party or an independent labor group. It could tap the support of other community groups which would have been very suspicious of labor operating alone. Under the party cover PAC was less vulnerable to newspaper attack as a special interest group.

Third, PAC was in a stronger position to promote its legislative program. It could expel from the party any groups opposed to labor's issues. It could see that labor's issues were publicized as Democratic issues and that candidates remembered them when once elected.

And, finally, from its inside position PAC had firsthand contact with state and national Democratic committees. It could help select delegates to state and national conventions—delegates with a firm organizational base in their local party.

But PAC discovered that its internal party position produced not only advantages but headaches. The first drawback was that it required considerable political resources. The 1950 victory was not permanent. Unless PAC kept money in its coffers and workers on the streets, it might be reduced to an impotent position inside the party in the next primary. In Chicago, PAC was responsible for the campaign of one primary candidate. In Rockford, on the other hand, PAC undertook the primary campaign not only of a state representative and a congressman but also of forty-five precinct captains. While in Steubenville political activity could be a campaign-time phenomenon, in Rockford PAC workers were involved year-round in party tasks: electing officers, expanding organization, disciplining internal interest groups, and distributing patronage. PAC could no longer concentrate on the party's "soft spots." It had undertaken party responsibility itself.

A second difficulty was that, in order to build its controlling coalition, PAC had to come to terms with other interest groups. The Steubenville PAC might limit affiliation to "those in accord with CIO objectives," but the Rockford PAC was forced to forego the luxury of untrammeled idealism in exchange for political resources. It worked with the All American Club, whose reason for existence was scarcely the promotion of labor legislation. Combining sufficient resources to win a general election will require even further compromises, which PAC may have trouble explaining to CIO members and the state PAC.

Third, PAC faced the difficult problem of maintaining its identity as an interest group inside the party. A PAC with its own precinct organization could do this easily. Its workers were obviously neither Republicans nor Democrats. If they were disloyal to PAC, they could be fired. But this was not true of PAC workers who were elected Democratic precinct captains. If jobs or reform or protection suddenly became more appealing to them than PAC issues, they were free to shift their party vote to other internal interest groups. PAC could do nothing about such disloyalty until the next election. In the community, PAC precinct workers became known as Democrats rather than as unionists. Their experience in political circles, where compromise was considered "intelligence" rather than "betrayal," often gave them quite a different outlook from their union brothers on the picket line. What was to keep these union precinct workers identified with PAC? The district leader sought to keep their loyalty by classes, caucuses, threats, and idealism. But, like all human beings, PAC workers were vulnerable. Other party interest groups were free to capture their support if they could.

A fourth difficulty was that CIO risked splitting its own membership by adopting an openly partisan position. CIO members had traditional party loyalties, and some of them were Republicans. Rockford PAC could no longer, like Steubenville, keep up the fiction of independence from both parties. It was Democratic.

Finally, an internal relationship with the Democratic party did not automatically get PAC's candidate elected. In the solid South a place on the Democratic ticket might be tantamount to election, but in rural Illinois it might well be just the opposite. An influential position inside the Democratic party merely meant that PAC faced the problem of creating a final election majority with the support, rather than the hostility, of other Democratic interest groups.

Why Did PAC Enter the Party in Rockford?

What made an internal relationship possible in Rockford, though impossible in Chicago?

The election district.—In 1950 Winnebago County accounted for 51 per cent of the Democratic votes for congressman cast in the entire Sixteenth Congressional District. Clearly, this county party led the Democratic political life of the district.

Like the Democrats, organized labor had few members in the rural counties. Eighty per cent of the CIO's district membership was concentrated in the industrial communities around Rockford. Organized labor formed a strategic bloc in a strategic county. Furthermore, PAC's votes were well distributed over this important county. They were not huddled in a few precincts, as in Steubenville. PAC could thus hope to elect a good proportion of precinct captains to the County Democratic Committee. This concentration of CIO members in a strategic election area favored activity inside the Democratic party.

Voting behavior.—The Democratic primary vote in Rockford has been low in the last ten years. With from 1,500 to 3,000 primary votes, PAC could expect to control the party. Even fewer votes were required to elect a majority of precinct captains. This did not look like an impossible request of Rockford's 14,000 CIO members or a coalition. Swinging a balance of power at a general election would require from 1,000 to 5,000 votes in Rockford and up to 22,000 in the Sixteenth District. Internal action in Rockford, unlike Steubenville, seemed to be the alternative requiring least political effort.

The Democratic primary vote in Rockford has been low, but the difference between the parties at the final election has been relatively high. In 1950, for example, PAC or its coalition could have controlled the Winnebago County party with the few primary votes needed to elect precinct captains carrying 3,178 votes. It could have won the primary contest for congressmen in the entire district with 5,543 votes. But it would have required 4, 758 votes to swing the final election in Winnebago County, and 21,123 votes to balance power in the district. In Rockford, unlike Steubenville, entering the party was the alternative requiring least political resources.

Compatible interest groups.—In 1950, PAC had to get the support of the All American Club even to control a weak county committee. Could it hope for enough support from compatible interest groups to defeat the Republicans? If a Democratic victory were really hopeless, PAC might better spend its political resources to make changes within the Republican party!

The AF of L had about 6,000 members in Rockford. Politically, however, they were inactive and divided. Some sided with PAC; others were said to have been captured by Republican patronage. Rockford has about 11,000 workers in retail trades, but in 1950 they had no interest-group organization. Labor was a potential, but still poorly developed, source of Democratic votes.

A few small businessmen had organized themselves and had given some help to Goldman. But their resources could hardly compare with the Republican-oriented Chamber of Commerce, consisting of 375 large firms and reputed to be one of the most active in the United States.

Like Steubenville, Rockford had nationality and ethnic groupings which might support liberal issues under a Democratic label. Almost half of Rockford's 92,500 inhabitants were of Swedish extraction. A majority of them voted Republican, but an important minority resembled the La Follette Progressives of near-by Wisconsin. In local politics this Progressive group ran a slate of its own. In state and national affairs they might well support a liberal Democrat.

The Italian community numbered about 5,000. Though small, it was significant politically because of its active political interest group, the All American Democratic Club. As indicated, PAC obtained the support of this group in 1950. Rockford's Negro community had over 5,000 members but little influence because of its poor political organization. Almost the only group contact which Goldman could establish with Negro voters was through the Negro Legion post. As in Ohio, Negroes were a potential, but undeveloped, source of Democratic votes.

Two gambling syndicates were said to be of political significance in Rockford. In 1950, political gossip claimed that both Republican and Democratic candidates for sheriff got campaign funds from this source. Contrary to Steubenville, the Rockford PAC openly proclaimed its incompatibility with protection groups. The Democratic candidate for sheriff got no PAC support. PAC did not intend to develop this possible resource.

With this lineup of interest groups and groupings, the PAC leader believed that action within the Democratic party was worth while. While the activation and orientation of such groups might require hard work and a period of years, a Democratic majority was within the range of possibility at least within Winnebago County.

The Democratic party.—The Democratic party of Winnebago County presented a striking contrast to the high-powered machines of Steubenville and Chicago. Its structure, composition, and activity left it wide open to capture by active interest groups or coalitions. In 1948 no one applied for 28 of its 146 precinct jobs. With only one vote in each of these vacant precincts, PAC could have obtained almost a fifth of the membership of the county Democratic Committee! Infiltration required few political resources.

In Rockford the structure of the party also invited coalition activity. The chairman, secretary, and treasurer all had an influence on party decisions. The important patronage committee could be divided between PAC, the All American Club, and liberal independents. This division of authority made coalition government possible, whereas in Steubenville and Chicago that group which could elect the chairman automatically became party "boss."

When PAC entered, the Winnebago party had no strong leader like Alexander, the party chairman of Steubenville who could combine the assets of various interest groups and keep factions under control. The party was composed of small patronage groups ready to cut one another's throats. In these circumstances it was relatively easy for PAC to form a coalition with the All American Club to oust Hunter. It did not meet a hostile united front, as it would have in Chicago. Factionalism facilitated PAC's entrance into the party. Entering and raising a voice in the Democratic party was a fairly easy matter in Winnebago County. The real problem was to strengthen this party to the point of defeating a Republican at a general election.

PAC objectives.—Like other PAC's, the group in Rockford accepted as its immediate objectives the issues laid down at national and state CIO conventions. It indorsed its candidates on the basis of their willingness to support these issues and their ability to win. This issue orientation did not mean that PAC members had no other objectives. A few of them aspired to become candidates and political leaders. Others could be brought to PAC meetings only by the prospect of a free meal. But still it was the issue objectives that were held in common. Anyone who hoped to "work up in PAC" knew he was expected to remain loyal in this regard, just as patronage politicians remained loyal to their "friends."

The particular issues which PAC adopted predetermined the groups to which it would appeal. It could not be "all things to all men," like a patronage group. PAC might expect to get the support of Negroes interested in a fair employment practices act but was bound to find itself incompatible with the Chamber of Commerce, dedicated to upholding the Taft-Hartley Act. Whether PAC can formulate an electoral majority on the basis of its particular objectives in Winnebago County has yet to be determined.

Whereas the leaders of the Steubenville PAC could most aptly be described as "practical politicians," the leaders of the

Rockford PAC had somwhat the air of crusaders. Like Willoughby Abner of the Chicago PAC, they felt that there was something more to political action than immediate legislative gains. They felt that the economic and political power structures of Rockford were largely in the hands of groups which were hostile, or at least insensitive, to labor. They intended to challenge these interest groups, not just to force concessions, but to wrest for labor a share of actual political control. To them this was a fight for democracy. They would not have been happy with crumbs from a party table at which they could not be seated.

This militant idealism was an important contribution to internal political action. It engendered a willingness to fight and the perseverance necessary for the hard routine of party work. It made the PAC leaders and workers who adopted this philosophy more resistant to capture by the offers of other internal party groups.

PAC structure.—While eight or nine of the fourteen CIO locals in Rockford had local PAC's, the center of activity was the PAC of the Rockford Industrial Union Council. This PAC had about one hundred members, representatives from local PAC's. Some of them were "drafted" by the district leader, others volunteered. The PAC leader could remove them at will. Rockford's PAC elected its own chairman and secretary-treasurer and usually met over Sunday breakfast once a month to plan or approve political-action decisions. Members of this committee were the chief participants in investigating candidates, activating local PAC's, running for precinct captain, conducting campaigns, promoting registration, raising funds, and performing election-day work.

Most of the actual planning and execution, however, was left to the district leader, Willard Allen. By an arrangement between the UAW and the state CIO executive board, he gave 75 per cent of his time to political-action work during the campaign. Often he was at the plant gates at six in the morning, speaking to workers as they started the day. He often returned home at midnight after showing *The Roosevelt Story* in some rural community.

The Rockford Industrial Union Council gave its PAC some financial aid, but little direct supervision. PAC's lines of responsibility ran directly to the state Industrial Union Council, which could approve or reject its plans for action, give it financial support, determine its issue objectives, make final indorsements, and appoint its congressional district leader.

Since ten of its fourteen CIO locals were of the United Automobile Workers, the Rockford PAC had a close, though merely advisory, relationship to the political-action department of that international union. The UAW sent political material to Rockford, arranged political-action conferences, and extended the help of its regional political-action director. As a result, Rockford's political-action technique closely resembled that of Detroit.

The structure of the Rockford PAC was suited to internal party activity. PAC had enough members to produce quite a few precinct captains. It had contact with the Detroit experiment. Its leader was in a strong position to discipline and guide the group, and the state PAC was willing to allow experimentation.

On the other hand, PAC's structure had defects. The impetus for political action came from two staff members rather than from rank-and-file unionists. Political action might well collapse if the staff were removed. Basic decisions were made at the state rather than at the local level. As Rockford workers gain political experience, they may want more control over the policy decisions that directly affect them.

PAC composition.—Like his brothers elsewhere, the average CIO member in Winnebago County was not acutely distressed by his political position. He had joined his union for economic rather than political reasons. However, the incessant dances, smokers, raffles, picnics, and excitement at Rockford's CIO hall tended to make him aware that he was part of a group. He sometimes found his name and picture in the *Advocator* and felt a glow of pride. As a result, there were more group stimulation and support in Rockford than in Steubenville, which did not exploit these social possibilities, or in Chicago, with its urban impersonality. Unionists did not feel that they were acting alone when they became political liberals.

Nevertheless, the average political worker on the Rockford PAC was not intensely aroused politically. CIO legislative objectives and plans for entering the party sounded good to him, but he did not relish the endless round of meetings, campaigns, and precinct work. The large PAC committee soon dwindled. Patronage groups like the All American Club could provide more immediate incentives for their workers. The average PAC worker was not an experienced politician. Before January, 1950, he probably had not known how precinct captains were elected, and he certainly had never expected to be one. Rockford sent its members to PAC and UAW training conferences. The state PAC research director came to Rockford early in 1950 to give eight classes on political issues. But politicians are the product of years of experience, not of a few hours of instruction. As yet, these PAC workers have not been tested on the strength of their identification with PAC. Can they be "bought off" by the patronage or issues of other groups? Will they follow PAC out of the party as readily as into it?

The greatest asset of the Rockford PAC was its leadership: the UAW staff representative, his assistant, and the PAC chairman. All three men had worked in Rockford shops and had earned their positions of leadership by firsthand ability to handle CIO workers in tense situations. Unlike the state leaders in Ohio and Illinois, they had daily informal contact with CIO members. Their leadership was personal. They held a militant idealism about their work. By virtue of a rough political education in the hurly-burly of UAW politics, they were practical, aggressive, and ruthless wtih their opponents. They eyed a political fight with something akin to enthusiasm and seemed well informed as to the characters of their opponents, having met them for some years on the economic front. These men stood out among the PAC leaders studied, in their willingness to execute as well as direct political activity.

Time was a pressing limitation for them, however. Political action was a full-time occupation, but the two staff members already had responsibility for servicing ten locals, organizing new shops, and conducting Industrial Union Council activities. The PAC chairman worked in a shop and was president of his local. All three were impressed with the importance of political action, but also with the danger of purchasing it at the expense of decreased economic services to their locals.

PAC, like the party, had its factions. Its most debilitating factional problem was settled in 1948 with the expulsion of the left-wing unions, but other factions remained. The two steel locals refused to send representatives or to integrate their membership lists with PAC. One UAW local president joined the Hunter faction, causing confusion among eight hundred local members. PAC was by no means a monolithic group.

For this reason, much of its campaign effort had to be directed toward CIO members rather than toward building labor's contacts with other compatible groups.

Summary

As a result of its first primary foray, the Rockford PAC was able to elect about one-fifth of the Winnebago County Democratic Committee. With the help of the All American Club, it was able to form a coalition strong enough to elect top party officers and committeemen and thus control the party. From this internal position PAC could turn its hand not only to electing party officers but to filling party slates and activating precinct organizations. It could reduce factionalism on the committee by reconciling one group and ejecting another. It could use patronage not as a reward for its own members but as a means for strengthening its coalition.

PAC infused new life not only into the party but also into the campaign. Devoting itself particularly to the campaign of the Democratic state representative and congressman, it raised more money, publicity, and issues than the Eighteenth District had seen for years. PAC's internal position had several advantages. Instead of supplementing a weak and hostile party, it could make the party active and sympathetic. Under the Democratic label, PAC could appeal to groups which would have hesitated to support organized labor directly. It could make its legislative program part of the party platform and could interject its ideas at upper levels of the party hierarchy.

But an internal position also presented problems. It required continuous and hard work, as well as compromise. PAC ran the risk of being captured by other party groups. Its partisan alignment looked bad to CIO Republicans. And, finally, control of the Democratic party was only the first round in the battle. A Democratic congressional candidate had little chance of final election in this Republican district.

PAC was able to acquire this coalition control rather easily in Rockford. CIO members were concentrated in, and well distributed over, a strategic electoral area. The primary vote was so low that it was easier to enter the party than to swing a balance of power. The community contained potential Democratic groupings, which, if activated, might make a party victory possible. Party structure allowed for coalition control, and the inactivity and factionalism of its internal groups laid it open to "capture." PAC itself had comparatively strong leadership and some feeling of unity among its 14,000 members, though it suffered from factions and its workers lacked experience. When the electoral chips were counted, PAC found that it had obtained coalition control over a county Democratic party.

VI *Michigan: PAC Enters a State Party*

ROCKFORD was a fairly simple case. The PAC of a single industrial union council entered the structure of a county Democratic committee and obtained a voice in party decisions as
part of a coalition. But could a similar internal relationship be
established at the vastly more complex state level? How? What
effect would it have on the party? Under what circumstances
could it be accomplished?

The Michigan state PAC in 1950 was an important member
of a coalition in control of the Michigan State Central Democratic Committee. This is a study of the relationship of these
two groups and of how they functioned in 1948 and 1950 to
elect their candidate, Mennen Williams, governor of a traditionally Republican state (see Fig. 4).

PAC Enters the Michigan State Democratic Party

In Michigan, as in Ohio, the Democratic party is controlled
by two bodies, a State Democratic Convention, held in the fall
of even years and the spring of odd years, and a Democratic
State Committee, composed of four members from each of
Michigan's seventeen congressional districts. The state committee handles party business between conventions. Since 1948
both the state convention and the state committee have been
under the control of a liberal coalition composed of the

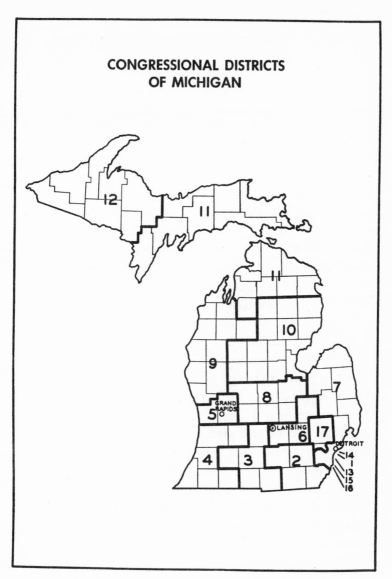

CONGRESSIONAL DISTRICTS
OF MICHIGAN

Fig. 4

Michigan Democratic Club, Reform Democrats, certain minority groups, PAC, and part of the AF of L. In the 1950 convention this liberal coalition claimed over 750 of the 1,243 delegates, about 486 of whom were CIO members. The 68 members of the state committee in 1950 were all from the liberal coalition, and 20 of them were CIO members. The story of how this liberal coalition came to power in the state Democratic party is so dramatic that it merits a chronological description.

The formation of the liberal coalition.—Republican Michigan had no permanent Democratic organization at all until early in the Roosevelt era, when a state highway commissioner, Murray Van Wagoner, formed a tight little patronage machine which eventually elected him governor. But, weakened by civil service reform, this machine collapsed in 1942, and party control passed to a small clique of Old Guard Democrats with a patronage outlook. Under Old Guard leadership, party precinct activity declined in the 1940's; party slates were not filled; the party exchequer ran a deficit; and Democratic candidates got little campaign help. Critics claimed with disgust that the clique did not really want to elect a Democratic governor because he might interfere with their control of federal patronage. Neither the platform of the state party nor the activity of the party in the state legislature reflected the New Deal orientaton of the national Democratic party.

This state party developed some dissatisfied factions. One of these might be called the "Reform Democrats," a few liberal party workers who strongly disapproved of the way the party conducted its functions and the associations it was developing. Another group referred to itself as the "Michigan Democratic Club," an issue-oriented group of depression-bred New Dealers who found the state party quite out of tune with the national party platform.

Meanwhile, a state PAC was established in 1944 as a committee of the state CIO Industrial Union Council. It dabbled unsuccessfully in third-party politics with the Michigan Commonwealth Federation. In 1945 and 1946 it developed its own independent political organization, usually supplementing Democrats. After a severe electoral defeat in 1946, PAC was in the mood for suggestions.

The leaders of the Reform Democrats and the Michigan Democratic Club provided the tip. One evening early in 1947 they invited the president of the state CIO Council to join them at the home of Hicks Griffiths, an active Michigan Democrat. In the course of the conversation, they convinced him that the objectives of all three groups were reasonably compatible and that their combined resources could control the party. This meeting became the birthplace of a liberal coalition which determined to enter the state Democratic party and seize control from the Old Guard Democrats.

PAC leaders had to convert CIO members to this form of political action, however, before they could pursue it. This took more than a year of internal CIO maneuvering. PAC leaders dwelt on the futility of third parties and the accusation of prolabor Congressman Dingell that PAC was "indulging in the luxury of non-partisanship at a time when a clique of fifty was getting control of the Michigan Party." They pointed out that labor was not large enough to spread its assets between two political parties and that nonpartisan labor usually found itself indorsing Democrats it had had no voice in selecting. They assured skeptics: "We are not accepting the Democratic Party in Michigan as it now is. Our purpose in going into it is to line up with its liberal elements and remold the Party into a progressive force" (*Michigan CIO News*, March 17, 1948).

On March 13, 1948, a state PAC conference in Lansing rewarded their efforts in the following declaration of policy:

"Progressives and liberals within the Democratic Party have often been outnumbered by conservative and reactionary elements. The PAC is unanimous in its opinion that the best way of supporting liberalism within the Democratic Party, to conform to National CIO policy, and to serve the best interests of Michigan labor, is to join the Democratic Party.

"It is our objective in adopting this policy to remold the Democratic Party into a real liberal and progressive political party which can be subscribed to by members of the CIO and other liberals.

"We therefore advise CIO members to become active precinct, ward, county, and congressional district workers and attempt to become delegates to Democratic conventions" (*ibid.*).

Walter Reuther gave his approval, and every state CIO convention since has reaffirmed this stand.

Building the coalition.—The first problem of the coalition was to build up its political resources. This involved bringing other compatible groups into the coalition. Part of the AF of L, the Brotherhood of Railway Trainmen, and important Polish and Negro political groups agreed to give partisan support. Some nonpartisan groups, like Americans for Democratic Action, the League of Women Voters, and a few liberal church groups, supported the new coalition, though they remained outside the party. The Teamsters Union and various Irish, Greek, and Italian political groups in Detroit lined up with the Old Guard Democrats against the liberal coalition.

Labor, Reform, and Michigan Democratic groups had to

strengthen themselves individually for partisan activity. The state PAC explained its objectives and trained its workers in specific techniques of partisan political action. It held innumerable conventions, PAC conferences, local union meetings, and classes. It started to raise funds. It sought to convince or control its own doubting Thomases, some of whom regarded partisan activity as dangerously radical, others who saw it as the megalomania of a few union bureaucrats, and still others who felt it to be a "betrayal of the revolution."

Meanwhile, other members of the coalition strengthened their own interest groups. Reform Democrats in a few places conducted their own revolutions and took over several county party organizations. Hicks Griffiths of the Michigan Democratic Club spent months traveling through Michigan, starting Democratic groups. His wife laid the basis for an organization of Democratic women. Mennen Williams, in his 1948 campaign for governor, visited small rural communities, not to turn out a big Democratic vote from these Republican strongholds, but to strengthen and liberalize Democratic organizations.

A second problem was to keep the coalition together. One common bond was discontent with the Old Guard party. Another bond was agreement on a liberal legislative program, including progressive taxation, civil rights, public housing, improved social security, and workmen's compensation. These points of agreement do not by any means indicate that the interest groups found themselves in complete harmony. Michigan Democratic Club leaders accused PAC leaders of being "arrogant," "politically naïve," and all too ready to shirk routine precinct work. It was hard for Michigan Democratic Club workers to see PAC workers paid for political work which they had to give voluntarily. PAC, on the other hand, found that it had to provide a good share of the money and manpower and yet eclipse itself modestly behind the coalition. It had to make concessions for the sake of unity, even when it was strong enough to enforce its demands. Each group suspected the other of secret "deals." But such conflicts were kept under control at frequent caucuses. Coalition members presented a common front to the Old Guard groups.

The final problem was to settle on a specific program of political action. The coalition decided to elect enough precinct captains at the bottom to control district and state party conventions. Old Guard Democrats were so lax in manning precincts and party conventions that this was a realistic possibility. But the plan required a tremendous amount of hard work, finding and training precinct candidates, raising funds, contacting interest groups, settling internal differences, campaigning, and poll watching.

Primaries and party conventions of 1948.—Each interest group in the coalition found and trained its own precinct candidates. Wayne County PAC, for example, asked all its union stewards and officers to run. PAC estimates that, of the 1,240 persons who filed for the 1,748 precincts in Wayne County in 1948, about 1,000 were from liberal interest groups. Seven hundred and twenty of them were elected.

The Old Guard was not expecting this challenge in the precincts. It failed to run sufficient precinct delegates to maintain control. At five of the six Wayne County district Democratic conventions which met shortly after the primaries, liberals easily captured control from the Old Guard. Coalition chairmen were elected for all the Wayne County districts except the thirteenth. Several other county parties also went liberal. State convention delegates were selected at these district and county conventions. Wayne County districts naturally selected liberal delegates, and this populous county happened to hold a majorty vote at the state convention.

The 1948 state convention was about twice as large as in previous years. A PAC official estimated that the liberal coalition mustered two-thirds of its votes. One informed Democrat claimed that PAC had majorities in four of the seventeen district convention delegations and was an important element in two others. PAC leaders admit that they had a "good proportion of the total delegates, but probably less than half." Clearly, PAC formed the largest single group within the coalition.

The coalition captures the state committee.—Since the State Democratic Committee is not elected at fall conventions, a member of the Old Guard, John Franco, continued as state party chairman. War raged between liberal and Old Guard members on the committee.

Liberal members called a 1949 spring party convention for February 5, and Old Guard members ordered it for February 25. Sparks flew. Franco tried to remove Griffiths, who was the obvious liberal contender for the state chairmanship, from the state committee. He claimed he would be happy if the liberals held their "illegal" convention, saying, "Then we would be able to weed out the socialist element of the Democratic Party." Liberals retorted that Franco's report of party contributions was $9,000 short and that he had paid a 45 per cent commission to his brother's firm for raising funds.

The liberal coalition proceeded to hold its state convention on February 5, with 1,243 delegates, far more than the Old Guard could round up. Griffiths, leader of the Michigan Democratic Club, was easily elected state chairman. Sixty-eight liberals were elected to the state committee, of whom CIO claimed twenty. PAC showed its muscle at this convention.

The *New York Times* of February 6, 1949, complained that "Scholle, rather than the governor, was real head of the convention." Scholle, director of the state CIO, responded: "Although CIO members constitute a substantial portion of the Democratic Party delegations, they do not operate as a unit" (*Michigan CIO News*, February 9, 1949).

The Old Guard insisted that they would hold another convention up until two hours before it was supposed to convene on February 25. Then Franco capitulated lamely, saying he would have certified the February 5 convention, "if the opposition had given him a vote of gratitude."

The 1950 primaries.—The liberal coalition thus found in 1948 that it could attain a position of leadership in the state convention and state committee by entering its members as precinct delegates. But could it hold this position in succeeding primaries when the Old Guard and other interest groups had become aware of this method of attack?

In February, 1950, an attorney for the Teamsters' Union started an Old Guard caucus known as the Truman Democratic Club of Michigan. Its object was to recapture control from the liberal coalition.

The coalition operated in 1950 much as it had in 1948, filing about 1,000 petitions for precinct captains in Wayne County, 821 of these petitions being from CIO members. But imagine the surprise of the liberals to discover that 3,598 persons had filed for precinct jobs in 1950 compared to the 1,240 who had filed in 1948! Such precinct competition was unheard of in Detroit. Obviously, the Old Guard had been busy rounding up precinct workers, and coalition control was in jeopardy.

The liberals examined Old Guard precinct petitions carefully and noticed some strange things. The signatures were very similar to those appearing on 1946 petitions, and the same

handwriting appeared at regular intervals. The coalition concluded that the petitions must have been forged by a few men
sitting around a table and copying old petitions. They therefore checked about eight hundred petitions by writing to the
signatories. Some of their letters were returned marked "deceased" or "moved." Other persons gave them affidavits that
their names had been forged.

Early in August the liberal state chairman asked the Wayne
County election board to disqualify these questionable petitions. But the board declared that it had "no legal right to
check the authenticity of signatures, nor the qualifications of
candidates." Liberals then turned to the courts, which might
have considered these as cases of personal injury to the persons
whose names had been forged. Instead, a county court judge
ruled that this was a political controversy which should be
settled by the state party convention. This decision was small
comfort to the coalition. By the time the state convention met,
precinct captains running on forged petitions would have been
elected at the primary, and the Old Guard would again be in
control of the state convention.

"Blood on the Pavements."—Interest in the 1950 Wayne
County primaries ran unusually high. The county reported
222,804 Democratic primary votes for governor, as compared
with 81,796 in 1946.

The liberals concluded that, since they could not prevent
precinct captains from running on questionable petitions, they
would prevent those who won from being seated at the district
conventions, where party officers were to be elected. To this
end the coalition equipped Wayne County district conventions
with "bouncers"; a liberal bouncer from the Fifteenth District
told the author that he was equipped with six men, twenty
clubs, and two pistols but was not called upon to use them.

Evidently PAC did not have complete faith in its bouncers. Unknown to other members of the coalition, it made a deal with the Teamsters whereby the latter would receive CIO support for its chairmen in the First, Fifteenth, and Sixteenth districts and the CIO would receive Teamster support for its chairmen in the Thirteenth, Fourteenth, and Seventeenth districts.

District conventions were held on the evening of September 19. The newspaper public was regaled next morning with stories of the Fourteenth District chairman, a liberal, who "presided with a baseball bat." George Fitzgerald of the Old Guard walked out of one district convention, telling newspapermen that he had "just watched socialism take over the Democratic Party by Communist processes." A delegate to the Seventeenth District convention whose petition was questioned was carried outside and proceeded to make a radio platter entitled "Blood on the Pavements." Actually, the challenged delegates were given the choice of defending their petitons before the district convention or of leaving. Most of them left. The coalition won all the six Wayne County district chairmanships except the Sixteenth.

The Thirteenth District convention illustrates what happened to the Teamster-PAC deal. Since this district had 256 precincts, 129 precinct captains were required for a majority. The primaries turned up 90 known liberal precinct captains, 75 of whom were CIO members, and at least 16 Teamsters. The Teamsters had agreed to support a PAC chairman in return for 4 seats on the 15-man district executive board. PAC therefore did not question petitions in this district, and the Teamsters and Old Guard Democrats were seated. The first vote was for district chairman, and the 16 Teamsters violated their agreement by voting for the Old Guard rather than for the liberal candidate. PAC was incensed. Fortunately, the co-alition had enough votes to elect a liberal chairman by a small margin. PAC immediately dropped its half of the Teamster deal, and the coalition proceeded to elect all the district party officers and 100 delegates to the state party convention. PAC's first move after the election of officers was to throw out the 16 Teamsters and 32 Old Guard members on the basis of fraud-ulent petitions!

The 1950 State Democratic Convention.—Most of the Old Guard, defeated at the district conventions, decided to boycott the state party convention. George Fitzgerald announced that he refused to attend a convention, the delegates to which had been picked with "storm troopers guarding the doors and the chairman presiding with a baseball bat" (*Detroit News*, Sep-tember 27, 1950). Mrs. Nellie Riley, a former Democratic National Convention delegate, warned her sex: "Socialists are in complete charge of the Democratic Party machinery. Mothers and housewives in Michigan cannot afford to let the state go socialistic" (*Detroit News*, September 28, 1950).

Shortly thereafter, most of the Old Guard interest groups turned to the Republicans! They formed the Democrats for Kelly Club (Kelly was the Republican candidate for gover-nor). The leader of this club said: "Leaders who have turned control of our party over to nonpartisans wth Socialist back-grounds and others of their ilk, cannot expect true Democrats to be complacent. I know of hundreds of good Democrats who feel the Democratic label is being used to advance ideologies to which we cannot and will not, subscribe" (*Detroit Free Press*, October 11, 1950). The state CIO president, Scholle, was evidently encountering completely different Democrats. He claimed: "The overwhelming majority of the regular Dem-ocrats have welcomed us into the party with open arms. They find no difficulty in working with union members on a wholesome and co-operative basis" (*Michigan CIO News*, March 3, 1949).

With the exodus of the Old Guard, the *Detroit Times* called the 1950 State Democratic Convention on September 28, 1950, "the quietist in years." Of the 1,243 convention delegates, the coalition had at least 750, about 486 of whom were CIO members. Twenty Old Guard members tried to caucus, and one delegate questioned the district conventions, but neither caused much disturbance.

The liberal coalition, with PAC as its strongest member, thus weathered its second election as a controlling bloc in the Michigan State Democratic Convention and Committee.

The Coalition and Internal Party Decisions

Unlike the Ohio PAC, the Michigan PAC thus shared a position of direct internal control over the State Democratic Convention and Committee. From this position, what influence could it exert on the internal decisions of the party? How did the internal life of the party change when the liberal coalition came into power?

Selection of candidates—In Michigan, legislative and judicial officers are nominated at a direct primary, but a number of state and county executive officers are nominated at party conventions. From its internal position the coalition had noticeable influence on both primary and convention nominations.

At conventions, liberal candidates were predetermined at caucuses of coalition leaders and were approved like clockwork. The lively "horse-trading" of Old Guard conventions disappeared. Old Guard elements deplored this limitation on their operations; so did some liberal precinct delegates, who wanted more direct voice in return for their precinct work.

PAC leaders claimed they used their influence in the caucus as follows: If two liberals were contending for nomination, PAC did not take sides. But it supported liberals as against conservatives. Sometimes, in the interest of party unity, it did not oppose conservatives; but it always fought an antilabor contender.

The coalition also carried weight in preprimary maneuvers. Its chief contribution was an effort to fill the primary slates. In 1946 eight state senators and sixteen state representative districts failed to run Democrats. In 1950, under the liberal coalition, Democrats ran in all but one senatorial and three representative districts. Even though they had little hope of electoral success, the coalition made an effort to run "sacrificial goats" in strongly Republican areas because of their value as a nucleus for Democratic organization.

Theoretically, interest groups operate separately in running primary candidates. Actually, the standards of indorsement for issue-oriented members of the coalition were so similar that these groups made an effort not to run against one another. Though primary co-operation was not so highly developed as in the party regular system in Chicago, PAC claimed that it would make no indorsement in a contest between liberals. At general elections PAC stated flatly that it would not indorse an antilabor Democrat or a Republican of any kind.

The result of this policy has been more liberal Democratic primary contenders, especially in Wayne County.

The state Democratic platform.—One of the most striking changes in the function of the Michigan state Democratic party under the liberal coalition is in the content, creation, and use of the state party platform.

Both the phraseology and the content of the 1948 and 1950 Michigan Democratic platforms indicated that the party, under the liberal issue-oriented interest groups, aimed its appeal at a particular segment of Michigan voters. It did not attempt to please everyone, as the previous patronage-oriented party had done. The state Democratic party platform stated: "For this record of indifference and hostility to labor's interests the Republican Party stands condemned. The Democratic Party believes that the prosperity of the whole state depends on the health, security, and dignity of the working man" (*Michigan CIO News*, October 5, 1950, p. 4). Furthermore, the platform stood for specific legislative items which patronage interest groups had considered too controversial: a corporation profits tax, improved social security, a fair employment practices act, workers' education, and public housing. PAC's hand in this platform can be seen easily by comparing the platform with the state PAC legislative program. This platform, like the selection of candidates, was actually determined at informal caucuses of coalition leaders. Ratification by the state convention was assured.

Perhaps the most significant change regarding the state platform, however, was its use. Platforms of 1944 and 1946 state conventions played little part in the actual selection of candidates, campaign issues, and legislative battles. Liberal caucuses, on the other hand, did evaluate potential candidates on these issues. Williams used platform issues continuously in his campaign. These issues were stressed in his inaugural address in 1949 and in his first address to his Republican-dominated state legislature. In his first term he conducted sharp legislative battles on workmen's compensation, discrimination in the state militia, workers' education, old age benefits, and public housing.

The Michigan party platform thus adopted a specific social orientation and became more binding, not because of any theoretical desire for "responsible" parties but because it had become a power medium for specific issue-oriented social groupings.

Electing party officers.—The influence of PAC and the liberal coalition in electing precinct captains, district officers, and state conventions and committees has already been described. The coalition elected enough precinct captains in Wayne County to control four of its five district conventions and a majority of the state convention.

Expanding party organization.—Under the Old Guard, party organization in the state rural districts had been practically nonexistent. The Michigan Democratic Club set out to remedy this situation. Griffiths founded liberal Democratic groups; Williams visited them in the course of his campaign. These small county Democratic organizations were encouraged to run candidates, even with little hope of success, as a nucleus for party organization.

Even in urban areas the Old Guard had let basic Democratic organization slip. In 1946 no Democrat ran for over half the precincts in Wayne County, whereas 3,598 persons filed for these 1,748 places in 1950. Under the coalition, Democratic organization spread at the "grass-roots" level.

Internal party discipline.—The liberal coalition ejected the incompatible Old Guard interest groups from the party by electoral means, supplemented in the 1950 district conventions by "bouncers." But what held the members of the coalition itself together? Many groups like PAC, AF of L, and Michigan Democrats were held by similar legislative interests. Patronage groups found that their objectives, while not exactly similar, could be obtained from the same candidates. All groups were united by a common desire to wrest control from the Old Guard.

What kept PAC from dominating this coalition? Certainly not timidity! PAC was limited by the fact that, while it had sufficient votes and money to dominate the coalition, it did not have sufficient resources to win a general election. In Michigan, as in Ohio, a liberal candidate had a far better chance of election when supported by a coalition with a traditional party name than he did with a strictly CIO label. The Michigan Democratic Club contributed liberal candidates and a state-wide organization which performed as much precinct work as PAC members did. Reform Democrats provided party leaders of considerable political experience, like Niel Staebler, the 1950 state party chairman. These nonlabor members of the coalition proved more resourceful than PAC in contacting and reconciling compatible interest groups. They were even instrumental in reconciling compatible interest elements in the AF of L. Since PAC needed help to defeat the well-intrenched Republicans, it was forced to broaden the coalition by compromise rather than narrow it by domination.

Distributing patronage.—PAC claimed it could get along without routine patronage jobs. It could pay PAC workers from union treasuries for time lost from work for political duties without the risk of losing them to the County Court House, and few workers wanted to give up factory pay and seniority for the insecurity of political jobs, anyway. But PAC and other issue-oriented groups evinced considerable interest in policy-making jobs. PAC did not hesitate to bring pressure for sympathetic appointees to the Michigan Unemployment Compensation Commission, the state Department of Labor, and the Public Service Commission. These, it felt, directly affected labor. When it became apparent that Governor Williams might appoint Vandenberg's successor to the Senate, all the coalition groups felt their interests were at stake and fought the matter out at liberal caucuses.

Michigan Democratic and Reform groups, however, admitted that routine patronage was of great use to them in building party organization. The Wayne County Democratic chairman felt that until he had more money at his disposal he would have to use patronage as an incentive. Griffiths of the Michigan Democratic Club claimed he found patronage useful in bringing Polish, Negro, and Italian groups into line. Party interest groups like the ethnic groups just mentioned found their chief party interest in patronage. Presumably more such patronage-oriented groups will enter the party if it becomes successful at county and city levels.

But patronage also had a way of creating trouble. District party chairmen asked that all patronage be channeled through them, for example. PAC, however, flatly rejected the idea of having its appointee for the Michigan Unemployment Compensation Commission subject to the approval of a district party chairman. PAC won this controversy.

In summary, PAC did not cease to exist as a distinct interest group when it entered the Michigan party. It merely entered a new sphere of political action. It could still be seen jockeying for candidates, platform planks, offices, and patronage inside the coalition. But neither did PAC capture the Democratic party. It had to share control with other interest groups inside the coalition in order to stay in power.

The Coalition Campaigns for Williams

The influence of the coalition was clearly displayed in Williams' second campaign for governor. His election in 1948 was not surprising. Democrats had held the governor's chair in presidential years with few exceptions since the depression.

But his re-election even by a narrow margin, in 1950 was unusual. Democratic governors had not been re-elected since the Bull Moose days of 1912. How did the liberal coalition handle Williams' 1950 campaign? What part did PAC play?

Fund-raising.—Since both the state PAC and the state Democratic party were campaigning for the entire state-wide Democratic slate in 1950, it is difficult to disentangle the expense of Williams' campaign from the others. Party and PAC sources indicate that total party and direct contributions to state-wide Democratic candidates amounted to $328,519.68 and that CIO unions contributed about $211,550.00 or 64 per cent of this (Table 4). The coalition thus relied on PAC as its chief benefactor. Michigan Democratic, Reform, Polish, and Negro groups did not have large resources, and the party's orientation precluded support from wealthy business groups.

CIO gave all but $6,000 of its contribution directly to candidates rather than to the state committee. The unions also made most of their contribution in the form of election-day workers and supplies rather than money. This enabled PAC to control the use of its money directly and to direct it toward developing its own political workers and orienting its own members. CIO thus used its funds not only to elect Democratic candidates but also to strengthen its position inside the liberal coalition.

Publicity and precinct work.—The liberal coalition built precinct contacts in order to enter the Democratic party. The same organization proved invaluable in campaigning.

The party conducted what it called a "grass-roots" campaign. It could not depend on the commercial mass media for support, any more than it had in Ohio. The 53 daily papers in Michigan were all Republican. Only 25 of the 350 weekly papers were Democratic. The *Auto Worker,* a United Automobile Workers publication, was the largest of these. Radio stations also had Republican leanings.

TABLE 4

SOURCE AND DISPOSITION OF MICHIGAN DEMOCRATIC PARTY
AND CANDIDATE CAMPAIGN FUNDS, 1950

Contributions to the State Democratic Committee*		Contributions Directly to State-wide Democratic Candidates†	
Source:		*Source:*	
Jefferson-Jackson Day Dinner......	$ 12,168.67	Michigan CIO Unions.........	$200,000.00
Williams Campaign Committee......	9,534.66	National CIO-PAC	5,550.00
Teamsters Union...	9,223.53	Nonunion Sources..	60,000.00
UAW-CIO........	5,000.00		
USA-CIO.........	1,000.00	Total..........	$265,550.00
Staebler..........	1,000.00		
Other............	65,749.38		
Total..........	$103,676.24		
Disposition:		*Disposition:*	
National Democratic Committee......	$ 35,317.67	State-wide Democratic candidates.	$265,550.00
Michigan Democratic Campaigns....	62,969.68	Total..........	$265,550.00
Balance on Account.	5,388.89		
Total..........	$103,676.24		

*Report of Democratic State Committee chairman to the Michigan Secretary of State (*Detroit Free Press*, November 29, 1950).

† Niel Staebler, chairman Democratic State Committee, interview, December 20, 1950. Tilford Dudley, assistant director, National CIO-PAC, telephone conversation, January 9, 1951.

Democrats therefore relied on the doorstep contacts of their precinct workers, on neighborhood teas, local square dances, and ward rallies. These were good devices for a group which suffered in the press but had a personable and hard-working candidate. Such a campaign both used and strengthened precinct organization.

In urban areas PAC played an important part in Democratic precinct campaign work. It loaned staff members ("co-ordinators") to act as full-time campaign executives for Wayne County district Democratic parties. PAC precinct workers were asked to contact all Democrats in their neighborhoods, not just CIO members.

Use of interest groups.—Another interesting feature of the coalition's 1950 campaign for governor was its use of interest groups. The Michigan campaign committee, unlike the Ferguson committee, deliberately concealed its interest groups. It had no special campaign committees and no labor representatives on the general campaign committee. Precinct workers approached all voters alike with the same broad coalition program. PAC precinct workers identified themselves, even to CIO members, simply as Democrats. When reporters called PAC for campaign news, they were referred to party headquarters. This was a hard role for a virile young interest group like PAC, which was footing bills, contributing precinct workers, and anxious to justify itself to its membership. But it was sophisticated politics even in Detroit, where "captured by the CIO" was often, as in Ohio, a political scare word. Unable to locate the CIO, Republicans concentrated on the Americans for Democratic Action (ADA), whose small membership still retained an exposed external position. In an open letter to the voters of Michigan, Kelly, Republican candidate for governor, said:

"What else do we have? We have a strange thing called ADA—I call it a 'thing' because I don't believe there is any other way to describe it. There has never been anything like it in the history of this country. It seems to be a collection of people who don't want to belong to any honest American political party, and who usually end up in their political thinking pretty close to whatever the Communist and Socialist party lines may be. The ADA, you will find, is simply another strange splinter group whose leaders are *hungry for power*" (*Detroit Free Press*, November 3, 1950).

But, though the Williams campaign concealed its interest groups, it had a definite social orientation. While Republicans denounced the liberal coalition as tools of the Kremlin, Democrats denounced Republicans as tools of the National Association of Manufacturers. Campaign publicity might have sounded like class warfare to Marx, but the fact was that the candidate for governor was heir to the Mennen shaving-cream fortune and the state Democratic committee chairman was president of an oil company!

Election-day work.—Unfortunately, Michigan has not been blessed with complete integrity in the conduct of elections. For some years politicians have been aware that everything was not always in order at the polls. In February, 1948, the Michigan Senate Subcommittee on Privileges and Elections studied senatorial races in twelve counties and reported irregularities. The coalition recalled this when Williams lost by a narrow margin, and they demanded a recount. Michigan voters were incredulous at the "errors" discovered. Some tellers had "forgotten" to count straight Democratic ballots entirely. Others had "inadvertently" counted the yellow oleomargarine referendum vote for Kelly. A vote canvass, completed on November 27, gave Williams a 1,154-vote edge. The Republicans then demanded a second recount on December 4 but called it off when Williams' lead reached 4,119 and after 3,400 of the 4,355 precincts in the state had been recounted.

The recount was expensive for both sides, and PAC helped

foot the bill of the coalition. The liberals thus performed a campaign function untried by the Old Guard Democrats. They helped police an election.

In summary, PAC actively campaigned under the Democratic label. Thus in Michigan, where organized labor actually played a significant role inside the state Democratic party, the average voter was scarcely aware of it. In Ohio, where organized labor had very little influence inside the party, many voters feared that PAC had captured the Democratic organization.

Advantages and Limitations of an Internal Party Relationship

From an internal position and with the aid of the liberal coalition, PAC was able to strengthen the party. Under the coalition the party took steps to fill its precincts, its slates, its conventions, and its campaign coffers. Thus strengthened, the party was able to re-elect a Democratic governor in 1950 under rather difficult circumstances. If it had retained its external position, PAC would have had to supplement a party even weaker than the party in Ohio.

PAC was in a position, second, not only to strengthen the party but to liberalize it. So long as the Old Guard controlled the party, PAC usually had to select its candidates from a "lesser of two evils." As member of a controlling coalition, however, it was able to use its internal influence to see that liberals ran in the primaries and were selected at conventions. It was in a position not only to enter liberal planks in the party platform but to see that they were taken seriously. It could eject conservative interest groups from the party and use patronage to strengthen the coalition. Instead of selecting between two hostile parties, PAC could help make one party a better vehicle for its own ideas.

Third, as part of the Democratic party, PAC received support from other interest groups which might not have co-operated in third-party or independent activity. The Michigan Democratic Club provided leadership. The ethnic groups carried votes in urban areas. Without such resources, PAC might not have been able to attain a share of control in the party, and it certainly would not have been able to elect a governor.

Fourth, whereas, in Ohio, PAC was exposed to public opinion as a special interest group because of its separate precinct organization and marked literature, in Michigan, PAC was hidden behind a broad party organization and a traditional party name. A Republican like Taft could scarcely have crucified Williams as a "labor candidate." Williams was a Democrat. His labor connections were not apparent to the average voter. Nor could Taft have capitalized on the idea that PAC had captured the Democratic party. The average citizen did not concern himself with district and state party conventions, and the interest-group composition of these bodies was not widely known.

But an internal position presented problems as well as advantages to PAC. In the first place, it required considerable political resources. In Ohio, PAC contributed heavily to one candidate in one campaign. In Michigan, PAC had to subsidize the party and a number of campaigns. Internal party activity was costly to PAC not only in money but in work. PAC had to locate and train hundreds of precinct workers, not just to supplement the party here and there but actually to carry party responsibility the year around. Successful internal activity also required a steady bloc of CIO votes. It is no easy matter to keep workers (or most average citizens) politically alert.

Second, PAC faced the necessity of compromise. Concessions to patronage, Reform, Michigan Democratic, or AF of L groups brought PAC under censure from some CIO members, who claimed their political organization had betrayed them or had been captured by the party. On the other hand, an uncompromising position would have lost PAC allies whose support was essential to control the party or win a general election. PAC's compromises had to be pragmatic, in terms of the balance of power at the moment. It could seldom take an "ideal" position.

In the third place, PAC faced the problem of maintaining the loyalty of its workers and members. Would the average CIO member remember PAC if he were approached only by Democratic precinct captains? How would CIO members who were Republican react to Democratic partisanship? Would PAC workers follow PAC directives, once in party office, or would they be captured by other interests? In 1948 and 1950, PAC successfully maintained its internal identity by dint of PAC training conferences, training sessions, caucuses, and idealism. Many, though by no means all, CIO members who attended Democratic conventions voted with PAC.

Fourth, could PAC trust its allies? PAC itself was not above a deal with the Teamsters, double-crossing other members of the coalition. Other coalition groups faced similar temptations to leave PAC out of new controlling party coalitions.

And, finally, entering the Democratic party did not automatically assure PAC of its ultimate objective—the election of sympathetic legislators. Michigan was strongly Republican except in its large urban areas. With considerable effort the coalition was able to elect a governor in an off-year, but his legislature was overwhelmingly Republican and could easily override his veto. An internal party position simply meant that PAC faced the general election with the support, rather than the hostility, of other Democratic interest groups.

Why Did PAC Enter the Party in Michigan?

Why did PAC in Michigan adopt an internal relationship to the Democratic party at a time when the Ohio PAC was building an independent political organization, even down to the wards and precincts?

The election district.—In Ohio, PAC would have had to capture a number of county parties in order to obtain control of the state convention or committee. In Michigan the liberal coalition had to capture just one—Wayne County. This county contains Detroit and 37 per cent of the people in the state. But Wayne County has an even higher proportion of the state's Democrats. Sixty-six per cent of the Democratic votes for governor in the 1948 primary were cast in the five congressional districts of Wayne County! A coalition which controlled Wayne County was therefore in a position to control the State Democratic Convention.

Fortunately for PAC, CIO membership was also highly concentrated in this strategic voting area. Four hundred thousand of CIO's 700,000 Michigan members voted in Wayne County. By political activity in one county where the CIO was strong, PAC could obtain a share of control in the Michigan state Democratic party.

Election practices.—In Wayne County, PAC could enter the Democratic party by electing precinct captains rather than ward leaders—a much less formidable task. The votes of these precinct captains actually controlled district conventions and the selection of state convention delegates. Michigan precinct captains were up for election every two years.

The Michigan PAC could thus enter the party at the precinct level, whereas the Chicago PAC could not.

Voting behavior.—The Democratic primary vote in Michigan

in the mid-1940's was low. In 1947 the coalition could count on nominating a governor with 100,000 votes, a figure which seemed within the range of possibility for PAC with Michigan Democratic Club and Reform group support. The primary vote also indicated easy access to the party hierarchy through the precincts.

The *Detroit Times* (September 27, 1950) described Michigan's general election voting behavior as follows: "Michigan has never been blessed with a strong opposition party. For three quarters of a century prior to 1932 it was a stand-pat Republican state. Since 1932 it has been a maverick; Democrats grabbing control in presidential years, and disorganized Republicans stumbling to recover in by-election years" (p. 30).

In 1932, 1936, and 1940, with Roosevelt heading the ticket, Michigan voters put Democrats in the governor's chair. The off-years, 1934, 1938, and 1942, as regularly produced Republican governors. But evidently the Democrats relied more on depression psychology than on basic party organization. With the coming of war prosperity, Democratic governors lost by 219,522 votes in 1944 and by 359,338 votes in 1946. This large difference between the Republican and Democratic vote in the mid-1940's indicated that PAC would have difficulty establishing a balance-of-power relationship. But the high Democratic vote during the depression indicated that Michigan might have a liberal vote untapped by the Old Guard Democratic party. The liberal coalition counted on this vote in estimating that it might revive the Democratic party. For this reason, Michigan's general election vote favored an internal, rather than an external, balance-of-power position.

Third-party activity has been a temptation to many Michigan CIO members. But third parties have never shown impressive returns on Michigan election sheets, with the exception of the Bull Moose party in 1912 and the La Follette Progressives in 1924. Father Coughlin's Social Justice party reached a peak of 75,795 in 1936; Wallace got 46,515 in 1948; Socialists never rallied more than their maximum of 39,205 votes in 1932. A successful third party is difficult to build in Michigan. It faces the adamant opposition of the press and a Republican party which can turn out 934,000 votes for governor. PAC did not have sufficient votes to make a third party a practicable method of electing a governor in 1950.

The low primary vote, the difficulty of balancing power, potential New Deal sentiment, and the poor showing of third parties, all pointed to an internal method of political action in Michigan. A coalition could enter the weak Democratic party through the primaries and make it a vehicle which might appeal to the potential liberal vote, without being placed in the exposed position of a third party or a supplemental interest group.

Compatible interest groups.—What interest groups were potentially compatible with PAC's program? What form of political action did they favor? With their combined resources, what forms of political action could liberal groups successfully underwrite? These factors had a bearing on the form of political action that PAC could adopt.

Some AF of L unions, like the Teamsters, had already attempted internal Democratic party activity but felt their objectives to be more compatible with the Old Guard than with the liberal coalition. The more liberal segment of the AF of L, however, at the instigation of the Michigan Democratic and Reform groups, agreed to give partisan support to the liberal coalition. The AF of L was not so active politically as the CIO was, but PAC could count on some AF of L support for partisan activity.

The Americans for Democratic Action, especially in Wayne County, was a small but active interest group. Though they refused to adopt a partisan method of political action, they agreed to support Williams and contributed considerable political work in 1948. A number of ADA members, like Williams himself, who became converted to the partisan approach, left ADA and joined the Michigan Democratic Club.

The support of Michigan Democratic Club and Reform Democrats was essential to the success of the liberal coalition. Their objectives were similar to, or at least not incompatible with, those of PAC. It is doubtful, however, whether PAC could have obtained their support for external or third-party political action. They were already committed to a partisan approach.

Especially in Detroit, the Democratic party has obtained steadily increasing support from Negro, Polish, Italian, and low-income groupings. Polish and Italian and, to a lesser extent, Negro communities had well-organized political interest groups with patronage objectives in 1950. Like the Michigan Democratic Club, these groups adopted a partisan relationship to the Democratic party. Hicks Griffiths approached these groups in 1948 and obtained the support of important Negro and Italian politicians for the liberal coalition. The political attachment of the Polish group wavered between Old Guard and liberal factions. It is doubtful whether these interest groups would have contributed their resources to anything but partisan activity.

Democratic party structure.—The Michigan party was controlled from the precinct level; hence its battlements could be scaled by electing precinct captains.

District and county party chairmen were not in a position of absolute control, as in Steubenville. They were supplemented by an executive board of fifteen members, which had more authority than the rubber-stamp body in Jefferson County. Since power could be distributed among party officers, coalition government was possible. The relationship of PAC to Michigan Democratic Club and Reform Democrats was not that of lord and vassals; party control could be shared.

Party composition.–Michigan Old Guard Democrats had not built a formidable machine with broad interest-group contacts, like the party in Chicago. Their ranks were decimated by patronage factions and the disaffection of Michigan Democratic and Reform groups.

As a result, party functions declined. Precincts and slates were not filled, factions were not disciplined, campaigning was weak. As in Rockford, the party was thus open to capture by a more active and disciplined coalition able to find and elect precinct captains and select and campaign for candidates.

PAC objectives.–The Michigan PAC, like the four others studied here, accepted national CIO legislative objectives. In addition, the state CIO council approved specific state legislative objectives and made indorsements on the basis of these objectives.

Like Abner and Allen, however, Michigan PAC leaders were thinking of more than a few legislative concessions. They had a vision of parties and governmental bodies in which labor had an actual share of control. Existing parties, both under the control of nonlabor groups, looked to them like Tweedle-Dum and Tweedle-Dee.

The Michigan PAC nearly had a civil war over whether labor could obtain this share of political control by entering an old party or starting a new one. The third-party idea was by no means a monopoly of CIO's left wing. Even while deciding to enter the Democratic party, the Michigan PAC left the third-party alternative open with the statement: "Resolved that a thorough and objective study be made of the results of this [partisan] policy in both primary and general elections in Michigan, with the understanding that if this program has been unsuccessful that Michigan CIO then recommend to the National CIO convention which meets in November 1948, that action be taken to unite the AFL Railway Brotherhoods, and other progressive groups for the formation of a new political party based upon a progressive political program and independent of existing political parties" (*Michigan CIO News,* June 23, 1948, p. 2).

*PAC structure.—*In 1950 the state PAC had 150–200 members representing county industrial union councils, CIO international unions, and state CIO and international union staff. This committee met quarterly to elect officers, determine policy, indorse state-wide candidates, and co-ordinate the political work of local unions and councils. Its members carried this policy back to their local groups.

As is common with such large committees, however, PAC policy was thought out by an executive board. The state PAC executive board consisted of about fifteen members: nine from the United Automobile Workers and one each from Steel, Chemical, Amalgamated Clothing, and Utility Workers' unions. All regional directors or international union presidents in the state were also included. This board met about once a month. Actually, however, its main work was performed by about five of its most active members, located in Detroit. This was the core of PAC leadership.

For its executive work, the state PAC had a staff consisting of a director, his assistants, five or six field workers, an education staff, a newspaper staff, and clerical help. Political action formed a major part of their work. Since the president of the state CIO Council, its chief executive, the chairman of PAC, and the CIO regional director were one and the same man, August Scholle, he was in an unusually strong position to direct political-action policy. He personally favored internal rather than third-party activity.

While the state PAC accepted the legislative program and presidential indorsements of the national CIO, its relationship to the national body was not close. The state PAC did not consult with its national office as to the form of political action it should take, nor did it keep the national body informed of its activities. Thus Michigan felt freer to experiment with partisan activity than did Ohio, which adopted a supplemental party relationship more in common with national PAC practice.

Under the state PAC were the PAC's of county and city industrial union councils. They co-ordinated and promoted CIO political activity in their areas but had to stay in line with state and national PAC policy on pain of disciplinary action. The state PAC was the center of power in this hierarchy. It was thus able to develop sufficient consistency of action to enter the Democratic party on a state-wide basis.

Composition of PAC.—The average CIO member in Michigan, as in the other communities, felt his union was necessary but did not hesitate to gripe about its political and economic demands upon him. Immediate CIO legislative objectives sounded good to him but did not arouse him to great excitement. Like his neighbors, he required considerable political education before he could be induced to undertake any form of political action.

Michigan's secondary leadership seemed to have somewhat more political experience and enthusiasm than Ohio's, owing perhaps to previous United Automobile Workers' excursions into the field of political action and internal UAW politics.

Their very awareness of alternative political objectives and methods, however, made factionalism a problem.

The bitterest factions arose over the issue of left-wing or right-wing control. The right wing won firm control of the state CIO Council in 1946. But the left wing continued in control of the Wayne County Council until 1948, when the national CIO took disciplinary measures to bring it into line on the Wallace third-party issue. Since Reuther's victory over the Thomas-Addes faction of the UAW and the expulsion of left-wing unions from the CIO, the right-wing has been assured of control of the PAC in Michigan. But the conflict resulted in the rather centralized and disciplined structure just described.

The greatest 1950 factional differences centered around the question of third-party versus internal party political action. This question was not premanently settled, and rumblings of discontent were not uncommon within PAC.

What were the political abilities and preferences of the PAC leaders in Michigan? August Scholle was state PAC director. He was militant, aggressive, and ruthless against opposition. His experience inside major political parties may have been more limited than that of some coalition group leaders, but he was well versed in the techniques of acquiring and holding power within the rough and tumble of the labor movement. He lacked Willard Allen's informal, genial, personal leadership, and he relied on authority, formal appearances, statements, and strategy to maintain control of his turbulent hierachy. He held the reins tight. With his own restless membership in mind, he did not hesitate to make sharp demands of the party in return for PAC support. The coalition did not find him an easy teammate. He was personally convinced of the effective-

ness of partisan activity and was largely responsible for build-
ind and maintaining it.

PAC thus had top and secondary leadership with sufficient
experience and control to attempt partisan political action, and
its membership was still in the stage of responding more readily
to Democratic than to third-party appeals.

Summary

In Michigan, PAC formed a liberal coalition with the Michigan Democratic Club, Reform Democrats, AF of L, and a few
patronage interest groups. By entering precinct captains in the
primaries, especially in Wayne County, the coalition was able
to control a number of district Democratic conventions and
send a majority of delegates to the Democratic State Convention. From this position the liberal coalition was able to determine the composition of the Democratic State Executive Committee. PAC was the strongest single interest group in the
coalition.

The coalition was able to bring marked changes into the
life of the Michigan Democratic party. It filled Democratic
primary and convention slates. It entered liberal planks in the
state Democratic platform and made the platform more binding. It governed the selection of party officers. It ejected the
conservative Old Guard. It used its influence to appoint liberals
to policy-determining patronage jobs and used routine patronage to strengthen its coalition. PAC's hand was observable in
all these changes.

The coalition also had new ideas about campaigning and
footed more than half the bill. Liberal Democratic campaigns
relied on precinct work rather than on large-scale publicity.
Special interest groups were well hidden behind a general
Democratic campaign committee. For the first time the Demo-

cratic party challenged a state-wide election and won a governor.

This internal position had obvious advantages for PAC. Instead of attempting to deal with a weak and hostile party, it helped create an active and friendly body. PAC's assets were supplemented by those of other compatible groups which might not have followed PAC into more independent activity. PAC was not left exposed before the newspapers. But an internal position also presented problems. It was costly in money, work, and votes, and it required compromises. PAC ran the risk of capture by other party groups or of being left out of new party coalitions. And, finally, a position on the Democratic ballot by no means insured a liberal candidate of actual election.

A third party was impractical as a means of electing Michigan's governor in 1950. Liberals were concentrated in a few urban areas, and their interest groups were already involved in a partisan approach. CIO members did not show themselves capable of a large independent vote, and their Republican opponents were strong. A supplementary or balance-of-power relationship also seemed unsatisfactory. The Republicans were strong, and both parties were hostile. PAC leaders wanted more than a "lesser of two evils." But the Democratic party was weak in the precincts and the primary and was made vulnerable by Michigan election law. Liberal groups were willing to co-operate in a partisan move. PAC was strong enough and disciplined enough to think in state-wide terms. In 1948 and again in 1950 it was therefore able to share party control. A coalition, with PAC as an important member, found that it was able to capture the state Democratic party.

VII   *Parties under Pressure*

PRESSURE groups may be labeled "good" or "evil," but they can hardly be called "parasites" on the party process. The fore-going five cases indicate that party pressure groups are made up of those people who, for good reasons or bad, care enough about their objectives to give life and direction to the party mechanism. Without such groups, the party could not exist. Without them, parties would lose their very reason for exis-tence as reconcilers of conflicting human interests. Even in small communities like Steubenville many such interest groups are observable, interacting with one another in a bewildering and ever changing array of pressure relationships.

Should these five case studies rest merely as separate stories, interesting only in 1950? Or do they point up some charac-teristic problems and possibilities facing any group which wishes to obtain its ends by electing sympathetic public officials? Do these cases provide any consolation to the harried voter, who wonders whether his party has succumbed to the "special interests"?

Pressure Groups and Their Alternatives

PAC's experiences in Ohio, Steubenville, Chicago, Rockford, and Michigan indicate that there is a number of legitimate methods of action open to an interest group which wishes to make its desires felt by a political party. Some of these alternatives are more influential than others.

Perhaps the simplest method is *advisory*. The interest-group leader need only dial a phone, buy the party chairman a drink, or testify before a platform committee, in order to pass along his suggestions to party decision-makers. This method requires no votes, no money, and little work from the interest group, but it does have one serious drawback. Party leaders are quite free to ignore suggestions. Mere advice, therefore, is not an effective means for promoting interests which conflict with those of the groups controlling the party.

A somewhat more influential alternative is for an interest group to *supplement* the campaign of whichever major party candidate seems most sympathetic toward its objectives. To do this, an interest group may merely make an indorsement on paper, or it may give everything it has in money, votes, and work, as PAC did in Ohio. Such a method may help elect a more or less sympathetic representative, but it must accept existing parties and candidates as they are. All a supplemental group can do is to pray that some party will produce a candidate worth supporting and a campaign worth mentioning. Such an interest group cannot help solve internal party problems.

If the interest group has enough votes for its support to mean success or defeat in a final election, it has established a *balance of power*. PAC was in this fortunate position in Steubenville in 1950. From this position an interest group can do more than supplement a campaign, it can command some attention from party decision-makers as they choose candidates, plan strategy, and distribute patronage. This is a position of some influence, but it rests on a chance occurrence—the major parties must be running neck and neck.

The direct primary has opened another method of action to pressure groups. They may now influence one important internal party decision, the selection of a candidate, by running their "favorite son" in the primary. A primary victory may be a cinch in a community like Rockford, where Democratic primary competition is practically nil, but it may require considerable effort and resources in a city like Chicago, with an active and united party machine.

Instead of building its own independent political organization to advise, supplement, balance power, or win primaries, an interest group may decide to enter and use the organization already created by the party. If it enters party structure, but with insufficient strength to control internal party decisions, it is in the position of a *party vassal*. While vassals may wield some influence through prompt suggestions, clever maneuvers, and hard work, they cannot expect to do much in direct conflict with the interests of the groups controlling the party.

But internal interest groups do not necessarily become party vassals, even when they do not have enough resources to control the party alone. In Rockford and Michigan PAC formed a *coalition* with reasonably like-minded interest groups. Together these groups could control the party. PAC had to make some concessions to these other groups in order to keep the coalition united, but the coalition was in a very influential position. It held the final word on all internal party decisions.

It is possible for complete control of a party committee to rest in the hands of one single interest group. PAC was not strong enough to achieve this position in any of the cases studied, but patronage groups had been able to do it in Steubenville and Chicago. Such *machines* require tremendous political resources, or else the help of restrictive election practices or an apathetic electorate. Machines are difficult to establish at the local party level, rare at the state level, and impossible nationally. But no one can mistake the influence of an interest group in control of a machine. It can make final party decisions single-handed.

Instead of attempting to influence existing parties by external or internal pressure, an interest group is free to challenge them outright by forming a party of its own. It simply runs its own candidates at a general election. Some small parties, like the Socialist party, nominate candidates without seriously trying to elect them. They are thus able to put forward men dedicated to clearly defined ideals, without making the compromises necessary to combine enough resources to elect them. Such *ostensible third parties* are not without influence in pointing out issues to major parties. But they cannot themselves elect candidates.

For generations, interest groups, especially of the liberal variety, have longingly discussed the possibility of a *serious third party*, both dedicated to specific issues and able to elect candidates. The thought is appealing, but the practical difficulties are tremendous. A serious third party would have to combine sufficient political resources to defeat the strongest major party outright at a general election. Unless it could tap strong new interest groups, undiscernible at present, the new party would have to come to terms with existing pressure groups. As a result, its program would soon resemble that of the two major parties.

Pressure Groups and Their Limitations

Various alternatives thus lie open to any interest group which wishes to make itself felt in party circles. Why does not every group select the most influential pressure relationship—say, a machine or a third party? Political life is not so simple as that. Every alternative requires some outlay of votes, funds, or political work. The more influential relationships require political resources far beyond the limited powers of most groups.

When a man buys a car, he must find out, first, how much it costs and, second, how much he can afford to spend. The same is true of an interest group choosing its method of political action. It must first estimate how many votes, dollars, and workers will be required to establish each party relationship successfully *in its own particular community*. If the group finds its strength concentrated in a strategic election district, like the Michigan PAC in Wayne County, it may find that internal party action is relatively easy. The same method would require far more effort in Ohio, where labor votes are scattered. If the local party has adopted the practice of appointing, rather than electing, precinct captains, as in Chicago, the group may find it virtually impossible to enter the party at the precinct level, whereas in Rockford this road to power required only a few votes. If the primary vote is traditionally low, as in Rockford, the group may be able to nominate its candidate easily at a primary. But if the primary vote is high, this alternative may require a considerable outlay, and even then be unsuccessful, as in Chicago. If the major parties run close at a general election, as in Steubenville, PAC may find a balance of power possible. But a similar method would be out of the question in the strongly Republican Sixteenth District of Illinois.

Interest groups do not operate in a vacuum. Therefore, they do well to calculate the strength of other groups in evaluating alternatives for action. The Michigan Democratic Club and the Reform Democrats in Michigan had objectives and methods quite similar to those of PAC. Together, these groups had sufficient resources to enter the party successfully. The PAC in Ohio could not count on such help. In Chicago, PAC would have been naïve to undertake primary activity without the support of the Independent Voters of Illinois. And, finally, an interest group does well to calculate the strength and activity of the parties in its particular community. "Dead" parties are easy prey. But where the party has a strong machine, as in Chicago, almost any form of political action is difficult. Coalition control is possible in Rockford, where party authority is divided, but unlikely in Steubenville, with its strong party "boss."

Such factors in the political environment put a "price tag" on any method of political influence. The interest group must then decide which method it can afford in terms of its own limited supply of voters, funds, and workers. Despite brave talk, most groups have surprisingly limited political resources. Actual political interest among group members is often very low. Even after all its fireworks, the Rockford PAC found that only 1,700 of its 14,000 organized workers actually got to the polls and voted according to labor's indorsement in the 1950 primary. Another limitation is in leadership and workers. It is hard enough to get a man to vote; it is practically a miracle to get him to ring doorbells. Even when a political worker is finally convinced, he must be given training and experience. Persons capable of directing skilful state-wide campaigns are really a rarity. Internal factions are another serious limitation on the resources of interest groups. Groups are seldom as single-minded as they appear to the outsider. PAC is itself a fascinating study of internal cross-pressures. Before the expulsion of its "left wing," the Michigan PAC expended most of its resources not in "hot" campaigns but in bloody civil wars. As soon as they publicize their objectives, interest groups find that they encounter another limitation. Their aims immediately delimit the sources from which they can obtain support. When the Rockford PAC proclaimed its interest in reform, it could hardly expect to receive financial help from the syndicates. And, finally, the resources of an interest group are limited by its ingenuity and energy in performing the routine tasks of politics: fund-raising, registration, publicity, precinct work, contacts, and election-day work. Many politicians like to discuss and direct these jobs; few like actually to perform them.

In brief, then, these PAC cases indicate that there are various possible methods of influencing the election process; some are more effective than others; and each requires a certain outlay of political resources, as determined by local conditions. Selecting a method of action is not a matter of determining what alternative is most influential in abstract theory. *An interest group operates at its best when it selects the most influential alternative it can afford with its limited political resources.* This is why interest groups are found in a bewildering number of ever changing relationships to political parties. This is why an interest group like PAC has not adopted one immutable approach. Rather, it adjusts itself flexibly to each community, in order to obtain the most influence from the limited resources it has at its disposal.

Do Our Parties Need Protection?

These cases may thus be of interest to pressure groups, but what do they indicate to the worried voter? Has labor really captured the Democratic party? Are parties simply pawns in the grip of mysterious, all-powerful, uncontrollable "special interests"?

First, it should be obvious from these cases that pressure

groups are not supernatural forces. They are nothing more or less than groups of human beings, often our own neighbors, who have enough interest in some political objective to busy themselves in the election process. If we find their goals disgusting and their conduct deplorable, as we often do, the effective alternative is not a pious sigh. In a democracy we, too, have the privilege of joining and creating pressure groups to challenge ideas we do not like and to promote better ones.

Second, these cases seem to indicate that existing pressure groups are not so all-powerful as they would like to appear. The CIO in Ohio claims that it has 1,200,000 members on political occasions, but it did not consider them capable of producing the 160,000 primary votes necessary to nominate a candidate in 1950. Even the impressive Chicago machine has been known to have internal rebellions. The famed purse of the National Association of Manufacturers has a bottom somewhere, and its popular vote has definite bounds. No group has unlimited political resources. None is utterly invincible.

Third, pressure groups, even in our laissez faire type of parties, are not uncontrolled. They are regulated by the often fierce competition of other groups, ready to take advantage of any weakness. When the Old Guard Democrats in Michigan failed to produce an active party, the liberal coalition stepped into office. Pressure groups are modified also by the necessity of formulating a majority. PAC had to make substantial concessions in its objectives to maintain the liberal coalition in Michigan. And, in the last analysis, pressure groups are also controlled by unorganized public opinion, which, if finally aroused, can, like a might wave, sweep any pressure group out of its party bastions.

Fourth, these cases show that pressure groups are not just unfortunate incrustations on the party process. They are the live steam that sets the party mechanism in motion. Americans should not be surprised to find a maze of cross-pressures inside their parties. America is a land of conflicting interests. The party is a legitimate battlefield, where such conflicts can be expressed, tested, and settled with a modicum of physical violence.

Does this mean that the average citizen can settle back comfortably and leave his party to the play of these "natural forces"? Our election system has suffered as much from the great number of citizens who are afraid to look into internal party politics as it has from the few citizens who are afraid that they will. The well-intentioned voter could perform the greatest service, not by calling for the suppression of all pressure groups, but by informing himself and his neighbors of the groups at work in his party, what they want, whom they represent, what resources they have, and how they operate. He should direct his political efforts accordingly, and, especially, he should feel responsible for keeping his own interest groups internally democratic.

Should we give our parties legal protection from the depredations of unworthy interest groups? Legal suppression and restriction of live pressure groups tend to threaten the basic role of a political party, which is to recognize, test, and adjust human interests as they are. The place of the law is merely to establish and impartially enforce just rules for the "party game." The present American election system would greatly benefit from the enactment of more equitable election practices and stricter punishment for illegitimate political methods, such as intimidation, bribery, and fraud. *The problem of the citizen however is not to eliminate pressure groups but to improve the quality of their competition within his political party.*

Appendix *National CIO Legislative Objectives*

The Eleventh Constitutional Convention of the CIO accepted the following national CIO legislative objectives for 1950:

Now, THEREFORE, BE IT RESOLVED, That in pursuance of these objectives, we call for the enactment of legislative measures including the following:

"1. Repeal of the Taft-Hartley Act and re-enactment of the Wagner Act with improving amendments. We stand solidly against any provisions which would impose the use of injunctions to break strikes or which would impinge on other basic principles.

"2. Strengthening and improvement of our social security program, including extended coverage, substantial increases in benefits, addition of permanent and temporary disability insurance, and an improved public assistance program.

"3. A progressive tax program which shifts the burden of taxes from those least able to those best able to pay.

"4. Enactment into law of the recommendations of the president's Committee on Civil Rights. Specifically we call for:
   "*a*) Passage of a Fair Employment Practices bill;
   "*b*) Passage of legislation outlawing poll taxes and other undemocratic restrictions on the right to vote;
   "*c*) Enactment of a federal anti-lynching bill;
   "*d*) Passage of measures to bar segregation in interstate travel;
   "*e*) Enactment of safeguards against racial discrimination in federal appropriations;
   "*f*) Abolition of the Wood Committee;

156

"g) Enactment of laws protecting aliens long resident in the United States and regularizing their status.

"In addition we oppose all bills and Executive Orders to limit constitutional rights of American citizens and curtail the right of organization and association.

"5. Extension of rent control for the period of the housing shortage.

"6. Passage of an adequate housing program for families of moderate income, with provisions for loans to housing cooperatives.

"7. Enactment of legislation to protect tenants in war housing from real estate speculators.

"8. Improvement of the Fair Labor Standards Act to provide a minimum wage of at least $1.00 an hour, and to extend coverage to all workers whose employment is within the jurisdiction of federal legislation. We believe that at least an additional seven million workers could and should be brought under the protection of the Fair Labor Standards Act.

"9. Development of an economic program which will promote and maintain a full-employment, full-production, and full-purchasing-power economy.

"10. Improvement of unemployment compensation and the public employment service through more adequate benefit provisions and extended coverage in a nationalized system.

"11. A national unified health insurance program.

"12. Federal aid-to-education, properly financed, and an effective labor education extension service program.

"13. Strengthening of the U.S. Department of Labor and the return to it of all its legitimate functions.

"14. Establishment of a cabinet-status Department of Welfare to coordinate the health, welfare, and social service functions of the government.

"15. Veterans' benefits adjusted to meet present high costs, and the enactment of an adequate veterans' readjustment allowances program.

"16. Legislation to extend the displaced persons' program and eliminate the discrimination of the 1948 act.

"17. A comprehensive forestry program, including direct federal regulation of timber-cutting on all timberlands.

"18. Support for the integrated regional development of rivers and natural resources, utilizing the experience gained in TVA.

"19. A farm program geared to a full economy, including reasonable price and income support, farm credits, social conservation, and improvement of rural living standards.

"20. Adoption of the International Trade Organization's Charter which extends the principle of reciprocal trade.

"21. Adequate appropriations for the Economic Cooperation Administration.

"22. Retention under full federal control of "tidelands" oil resources.

"23. Defeat of proposals to protect monopolistic basing-point practices from action by the Federal Trade Commission.

"24. Approval of the St. Lawrence Seaway and Power Project.

"25. Enactment of legislation with appropriate safeguards to implement President Truman's "Point Four" proposal for assistance in the development of human and technical resources of under-developed countries.

"26. Provisions for the development and maintenance of a U.S. merchant marine of size and status commensurate with this country's role of leadership in world affairs."

In addition, the CIO voted to support legislation which would affect certain electoral procedures:

"We call upon all members of the CIO in all parts of the country to work and fight, through their political action committees, for legislation that will:

"1. Revise our registration laws to eliminate cumbersome requirements designed to prevent the expression of the popular will and provide only so much regulation as is necessary to prevent fraud.

"2. Pay state legislators and state officials enough so that able men and women and young men and women, anxious to make their contribution to the political life of their community, may be attracted to the service of the people.

"3. Provide for direct and open primaries in which all the people can choose the candidates for public office and in which all persons desiring to become candidates can file without undue restrictions.

"4. Remove from our political life the disgraceful practice of juggling election districts—both state and national—whereby voters in one community exercise more influence than voters in another and where representatives of a few hundred thousand people can out-vote millions.

"It is our further belief that the American democratic process, now undergoing its trial by moral strength with totalitarian ideologies that degrade and destroy human values, must be further strengthened by legislative action to:

"1. Eliminate the outmoded electoral college and provide for direct election of President and Vice President so that there will be no danger that a minority candidate can gain office by a technicality.

"2. Abolish the seniority system in Congress by which wisdom is stifled and age takes precedence over ability.

"3. Abolish the Senate filibuster."

Selected Bibliography

AMERICAN POLITICAL SCIENCE ASSOCIATION. "Towards a More Responsible Two-Party System: A Report of the Committee on Political Parties," *Americal Political Science Review*, Suppl., XLIV, No. 3 (September, 1950), Part 2.

BENTLEY, A. F. *The Process of Government*. Chicago: University of Chicago Press, 1908.

BINKLEY, WILFRED E. *American Political Parties: Their Natural History*. New York: Alfred A. Knopf, 1943.

BLAISDELL, D. C. *Economic Power and Political Pressures*. ("Temporary National Economic Committee, Investigation of the Concentration of Economic Power Monographs," No. 25.) Washington: Government Printing Office, 1941.

CANTRIL, HADLEY. *The Psychology of Social Movements*. Princeton: Princeton University Press, 1941.

DRAKE, ST. CLAIR. *Black Metropolis: A Study of Negro Life in a Northern City*. New York: Harcourt, Brace & Co., 1945.

FORTHAL, SONYA. "The Precinct Worker," *Annals*, Suppl. on "Parties and Politics," CCLIX (September, 1948), 30.

GAER, JOSEPH. *The First Round*. New York: Duell, Sloan, & Pearce, 1944.

GOSNELL, HAROLD F. *Machine Politics: Chicago Model*. Chicago: University of Chicago Press, 1937.

———. *Negro Politicians: The Rise of Negro Politics in Chicago*. Chicago: University of Chicago Press, 1935.

HERRING, E. P. *The Politics of Democracy*. New York: W. W. Norton & Co., 1940.

HUNTINGTON, SAMUEL P. "The Election Tactics of the Non-partisan League," *Mississippi Valley Historical Review,* XXXVI (March, 1950), 613.

KESSELMAN, L. C. *The Social Politics of FEPC: A Study in Reform Pressure Movements.* Chapel Hill: University of North Carolina Press, 1948.

KEY, V. O., JR. *Politics, Parties, and Pressure Groups.* New York: Thomas Y. Crowell Co., 1942.

———. *Southern Politics in State and Nation.* New York: Alfred A. Knopf, 1949.

LERNER, MAX. "The Outlook for a New Party Alignment," *Virginia Quarterly,* XXV (spring, 1949), 179.

McCUNE, WESLEY. *The Farm Bloc.* Garden City, N. Y.: Doubleday, Doran & Co., Inc., 1943.

MACIVER, R. M., and PAGE, C. H. *Society: An Introductory Analysis.* New York: Rinehart & Co., Inc., 1949.

McKEAN, D. D. *The Boss: The Hague Machine in Action.* Boston: Houghton Mifflin Co., 1940.

———. *Party and Pressure Politics.* Boston: Houghton Mifflin Co., 1949.

MICHELS, ROBERT. *Political Parties: A Study of the Oligarchical Tendencies of Modern Democracy.* New York: Hearst's International Library Co., 1915.

NYGAARD, N. E. *Twelve against the Underworld.* New York: Hobson Book Press, 1947.

ODEGARD, P. H. *Pressure Politics: The Story of the Anti-saloon League.* New York: Columbia University Press, 1928.

SCHATTSCHNEIDER, E. E. *Party Government.* New York: Rinehart & Co., 1942.

———. "Pressure Groups versus Political Parties," *Annals,* Suppl. on "Parties and Politics," CCLIX (September, 1948), 17–23.

STURMTHAL, ADOLF. *The Tragedy of European Labor, 1918–1939.* New York: Columbia University Press, 1943.

TRUMAN, DAVID B. *The Governmental Process.* New York: Alfred A. Knopf, 1951.

U.S. Congress., House Select Committee on Lobbying Activities. *General Interim Report Pursuant to H.R. 298.* 81st Cong., 2d sess. Washington: Government Printing Office, 1950.

———. House Special Committee on Un-American Activities. *Report on the CIO Political Action Committee: Pursuant to H.R. 1311.* 78th Cong., 2d sess. Washington: Government Printing Office, 1944.